L E A T H E R

PREPARATION AND TANNING
BY TRADITIONAL METHODS

Lotta Rahme
&
Dag Hartman
(chemistry sections)

Translated from the Swedish
by
David Greenebaum

Jack C. Thompson, Editor

Printed and bound in the United States of America.

ISBN: 1-887719-00-8

Library of Congress Catalog Number: 95-71505

Illustrations by Lotta Rahme & Carl Furfaro
unless otherwise noted. Photos by Lotta Rahme
Photo of Ms. Rahme on back cover by Susanne Costelius

Illustrations from: *A History of Technology*, v. II, by
J.W. Waterer used by permission of Oxford Univ. Press

Printed on acid-free paper

http://www.teleport.com/~tcl
For a complete catalog of books & videotapes

TABLE OF CONTENTS

FOREWORD

This book is a reworked and expanded version of the pamphlet, *Tanning and Preparation of Hides and Leather by Traditional Methods*, which was written in 1985.

Since then I have learned many new things, met many tanners and had the chance to work together with Inuit (Eskimo) and Indian women. In 1987 I set up a little tannery, where I tan and prepare leather and create clothing and other objects, especially for use in museums. In this book I discuss the methods of tanning and preparation which were in use before tanning with chrome and synthetic tanning agents became common.

There are still many people who possess great knowledge in the tanner's profession, but the traditional ways of dealing with leather are in the process of disappearing. In Sweden it is mainly with the Sami that we can find them preserved. Even the Inuit and Indian women I met in Canada complain that the knowledge will disappear with their generation, that the young are not interested in learning it.

Leather is a living material and nothing else is quite like it. A great part of the secret to creating a good piece of leather lies in a sensitivity of the hands. One simply cannot learn the experiences by reading, but rather they must be acquired through practice. All of the tanners I have visited have had their own methods and equipment.

The recipes which are jotted down in the book are based on my own experiences. It is my hope that the book can be used as a practical guide and will encourage the reader to conduct his own experiments.

A warm thank you to all who helped me write this book:
Dag Hartman, with whom I took my study trips and who helped me lay down a foundation for the chemistry sections. René Larsen, at the Conservation School [Konservatorskolen] in Copenhagen, who put forth great effort in checking the manuscript. The tanner Rudolf Frank, who shared his knowledge with me and lent me invaluable literature. The tanner Arvid Karlstrand, who lent me the use of many valuable tanner's tools and who taught me much. The tanner Erik Flink, the tanner Henning Hovander, Perjos Lars Halvarsson, tanning chemist Karl-Otto Geweniger, Institutet för Forntida Teknik [the Institute for Ancient Technology], all my students, and Kerstin Persson, who all supported me and patiently answered my questions.

Lastly, everyone at LÅS, the Inland Development Foundation, who put a workshop at my disposal and who were my fellow workers during the writing.

Lotta Rahme

There is an old Chinese saying to the effect that no good deed goes unpunished, and Alfred Stromquist did a good deed. On the 13th of July, 1992, he visited Lotta Rahme at her studio in Sweden and she signed a copy of her book for him. Upon his return to Portland, Oregon, he showed the book to me and I thought it might be of some interest to an English speaking audience. By mail, I contacted Ms. Rahme and negotiated the English language rights to her book; *via* e-mail I contacted the Medieval Text listserv and through the good offices of Professor Dan Melia was put in touch with David Greenebaum, who did a fine job of translating Ms. Rahme's text from Swedish to English. Al, who has studied the Swedish language assisted me as I edited David's translation. As the translation progressed it became necessary to consult people with a knowledge of Swedish and Chemistry. Three people came to my aid.

Claes Lindblad, of Lund, Sweden, got in touch with a Swedish chemist who was able to clear up a couple of points regarding chemical terms. Cecilia Usher was raised in Sweden and studied chemistry there, and Jeffrey Cawley, whose undergraduate and graduate work was in chemistry also reviewed the chemistry sections and provided useful advice. Carl Furfaro applied his excellent drafting skills to render a number of illustrations used in the last half of the book.

By 1995 the basic work had been done and all that remained was to scan the illustrations, and lay out the pages for the printer. But then I moved the conservation laboratory and the printer went out of business. The next printer selected wanted the text in a different format than the first printer and this meant going back to the beginning of the process. Other matters were more important at the time so this book sat on a back burner until now. While laying out the text and illustrations this time, I decided to include photographs, which I believe improves the book.

Rick Cavasin, an excellent parchment maker from Ontario, Canada, had attended one of the Technology of the Medieval Book workshops which I co-instruct in Idaho. He saw an early version of the text and continued to press me to finish the work.

Together with Allan Thenen, of St. Paul, Minnesota, Rick reviewed the final text and suggested improvements. He was also kind enough to provide the review which appears on the back cover.

Jack C. Thompson
Portland, Oregon
September, 1998

Originally, I had not intended to include a preface of my own in this book. I came to the job of translating Ms. Rahme's work armed with a knowledge of Swedish, but with hardly any understanding of the methods and vocabulary of tanning; I didn't feel qualified to express any sort of opinion. But although I ended up pestering Mr. Thompson (and through him, Ms. Rahme) with a barrage of questions, I feel that this book has given me a good basic understanding of traditional leather tanning.

I would like to thank Professors Dan Melia and John Lindow of the University of California, Berkeley; Max Shapiro; and the Reference Departments at Monroe County Public Library and Indiana University Libraries, Bloomington. Most especially, though, thanks to Lotta Rahme and to Jack Thompson for their help and support, and for seeing me through in spite of a difficult beginning. I enjoyed the work, and the new learning experience it afforded me.

David Greenebaum
Bloomington, Indiana
December, 1994

HISTORY

The use of hides and leather goes far back in the history of humanity. Finds which have been made from Neanderthal Man, *Homo Sapiens Neanderthalensis* (clever man), who lived about 70,000 years ago, indicate that they used stone tools to prepare leather {fig. 1}. However, there are no finds of skins or leather from this time.

Fig. 1. Over 100,000 years ago in France, a flint working technique evolved which was named after the location of the find--Moustérien. With the help of this technique scrapers were made which were used to clean hides. The new method involves striking and working flakes from stone cores (Drawing made after Leakey, 1981:135).

Fig. 2. Flint chips from the late paleolithic. At left a flint scraper, top center a drill, bottom center and at right flint points (Drawing made after Sklenar, 1989:21).

About 40,000 years ago there appeared a man of the subspecies we belong to, *Homo Sapiens Sapiens* (modern man). Thanks to a refined flint working technique, these hunters could expand their equipment, manufacturing new, more effective tools {fig. 2}.

They spread farther and farther north and managed well even in the cold arctic areas. These people, just as we who are alive today, were suited to life at about 27°C (80°F) and needed some form of shelter to survive in a colder climate. As soon as people began hunting for food, hides were an available resource for dwellings and clothing. It is probable that hides were used at first without any sort of real tanning. Man cleaned the skins of dirt and fat and then softened them mechanically, a method which is still used today by the Inuits, among others.

Tanning Methods

In time it was discovered that skins which had only been softened mechanically broke down quickly, especially in warm and humid climates.

1

Tanning agents began to be used to lengthen the skins' life. The first tanning method was probably oil-tanning. Our forefathers discovered the softening effect fatty agents had on our own skin. People learned from that and began to supply skins with extra, probably animal, fats.

Smoke-tanning is also a technique with an ancient lineage. People noticed that hides in dwellings were preserved by the smoke from the hearth and so began to smoke the skins which would be used for clothing.

In Egypt searchers have found "what is probably the oldest existing vegetable-tanned leather, tanned more than five thousand years ago" (Gansser 1950:2943). Vanity has been suggested as a cause of the discovery of vegetable tanning. Many vegetables contain both strong dyeing agents and tanning agents. It is possible that someone painted patterns on hides and eventually noticed that the parts which had been painted became softer and more durable than the unpainted parts.

In some areas, fresh hides are dried by rubbing them with salty earths which both draw out the moisture and have a bacteriostatic effect. If the earth contains aluminum salt, which is found, for example, in the Middle East, Africa and Asia, we get a type of alum tawing, which was surely noticed early on. "By the third millennium B.C., alum tawing was known in Egypt" (Bertel, 1949:31).

The various methods of tanning are described in detail later on in the book.

Equipment

A majority of the tools used in leather production in prehistoric times were probably made from bones. Unfortunately, few of these have been preserved, because bone objects decompose quickly, especially in calcium-poor areas. European finds of bone tools from the paleolithic* period show clear signs of having been used for leather working {fig. 3}.

A

B

C

Fig. 3. Scrapers for removing hair from hide,
a. of bone, with sharpened edge, paleolithic;
b. of iron, found at Pompeii (before A.D. 79);
c. modern steel scraper.
(Waterer, 1956:148).

"The curved shapes of some of these suggest that skins were scraped over a tree-trunk corresponding to the tanner's beam of later times. The form of these early bone implements appears to be perpetuated in the de-hairing and scraping knives of the ancient civilizations and of the present day." (Waterer, 1956:147).

2

We know that the Indians of Canada used split shinbones to scrape the hair side of reindeer hides for the production of chamois leather. Today we find that the same peoples still use tools made from the metatarsal bones of moose. These are used to "chop" away membrane and flesh from the stretched moose hide. Tools which may have been used in a similar way are also found in Nordic prehistoric material {fig. 4}.

Fig. 4. Bone scraper found in the Bäckaskog grave in Skåne[Scania], dated to about 5,000 B.C., length 30 cm (about 12") (SHM 22438).

In the Nordic area, however, most of the archaeological finds of scrapers from the stone age are made of flint, though quartz, quartzite and slate also appear. The oldest finds in Sweden are from the Alleröd Age (10,900-9,100 B.C.). Among them are scrapers from the Segebro settlement outside of Malmö. These scrapers were probably hafted {figs. 5a, b, c}.

Fig. 5a. Drawn after flint tool from the Segebro settlement outside of Malmö (Drawn from Burenhult, 1982:53).

Fig. 5b. Eskimo scraper with spruce handle from Point Hope, Alaska (Mason, 1891, Plate LXXVII).

Fig. 5c. Stone scraper with wooden handle, Chucherna (Drawing made after Bogoras, 1975:218).

3

In Norway and Norrland, so-called "krumknivar" (bent knives) of slate show up. These resemble the knives the Inuit use which are called "Ulo" (knives, or women's knives) {fig. 6}. At present, the oldest finds date to about 5,000-4,000 B.C. {fig. 7}. Copies of "krumknivar" have been made and proven very effective in flaying hides.

Fig. 6. Ulo.

Fig. 7. Slate "krumkniv"
(Broadbent, 1982:89).

During the Bronze Age, stone and bone scrapers were still used; it was not until the Iron Age that metal scrapers began to be used.

The oldest surviving iron scrapers have a shape which corresponds well with the woman's knife, Ulo. The S-shaped scraper is mostly used by the Sami today {fig. 8}.

Fig. 8. S-shaped scraper from Tisjön, Öviken, Lima parish, Dalarna. 7.9 cm (about 3") long. Dated to the Age of Migration, 400-550 A.D. (SHM 26485:V).

4

Pictorial Representations

In the search for information about the history of leather garments, we can study the sculptures and inscriptions which prehistoric man left behind. The little--about 5 cm (2")--ivory sculpture found in Siberia {fig. 9a}like the inscription in the cave in Gabillou cave, France, {fig. 9b}, shows us people who seem to be clothed in garments of furs with raised hoods, while small stone sculptures {fig. 9c} from Ukraine appear to wear garments of a different cut altogether. The sculptures are dated to about 20,000-15,000 B.C.

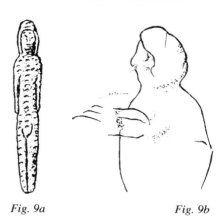

Fig. 9a   *Fig. 9b*

Fig. 9c

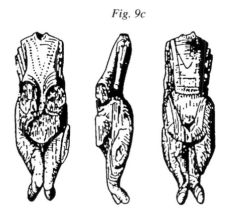

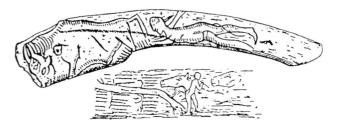

Fig. 10.   Bone carvings from Laugerie Basse (Backman, 1911: 278).

Figure 10 shows an inscription from the same period. "The fine hatching on the bison-ox, interpreted as fur, appears again on the man and may thus indicate that he wears a sort of leather garment with the hair side outward. The tail-like appendage which drapes over the man's leg could then be the remaining tail from the animal out of which the garment was made, which would be reminiscent of the custom of many primitive peoples. The lower picture shows a naked man" (Backman, 1911: 278).

Fig. 11. 'Trousers' and 'skirts' of skin. From wallpaintings of the upper Palaeolithic in the caves Els Secans near Mazaleon, Teruel, and Cogul near Lerida, Spain. (Waterer, 1956: 148).

In the mountains of eastern Spain, there are rock-paintings which reveal many details about the clothing of people of their time {fig. 11}.

The paintings belong to the so-called Levant Group and date to 8,000-5,000 B.C. "The women often have skirts and are bare above the waist. The men are generally naked, but sometimes have short knee-length breeches and various kinds of sash. This art can without doubt be ascribed to a hunting people who lived cut off from the sea in the mountainous country of eastern Spain." (Jelinek, 1978: 493).

Wall paintings depicting a tannery and shoe-making workshop can be seen in Thebes, Egypt {figs. 12a, b}.

We see evidence that the art of tanning and dyeing leather was well-developed in Egypt in the second century B.C. in a sandal, probably alum tawed, from Balabish {fig. 13}.

6

Fig. 12a. Egyptian leather-dressers. (Left to right) Dressing a panther skin in a jar; cutting with a half-moon knife; 'slicking' a skin; and staking over a 'horse'; shields covered with skin can be seen near the jar. From the tomb of Rekhmire, Thebes, c 1450 B.C. (Waterer, 1956:150).

Fig. 12b. Egyptian sandal-makers. (Left to right) Making holes in the side-lugs for the straps; pulling through the toe-strap which is knotted under the sole; cutting out the leather with a half-moon knife. From the tomb of Rekhmire, Thebes, c 1450 B.C.(Waterer, 1956:162).

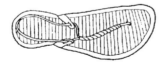

Fig. 13. Outline sketch of a sandal found at Balabish. Second millenium B.C. (Waterer, 1956: 151).

7

Clothing finds

One of the few prehistoric leather finds which has been made in Sweden comes from Västergötland, Redväg district, N. Åsarp parish, St. Fagerås marsh. In 1933, in the process of turf-cutting, "pieces of one or several calfskin 'bits of clothing.' were found. Some larger pieces sewn together from smaller bits with extremely fine leather thongs or sinews, some bits have edges which were originally sewn together and one fragment terminates in an end with a cord, made from strips threaded through a slotted part of the garment. On most of the bits, the hair is preserved." (Vitterhetsakademiens årsbok, 1936-1938, XXXVII Abb 3) The find dates to the centuries before Christ {fig. 14}.

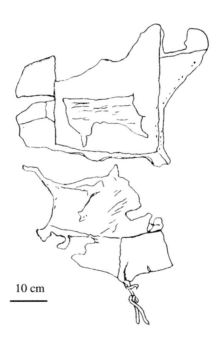

10 cm

Fig. 14. Find from St. Fagerås marsh, Västergötland (SHM 20709).

Another interesting find comes from Denmark. "In 1857, a find was made in Møgelmose, Jelling parish, Torrild district in Denmark, of a child who wore a women's jacket of leather ... The jacket consists of six larger bits of leather and two gussets." (Hald, 1980: 36, 355) The find dates to circa 200 B.C. and the leather is thought to come from a woods-marten {fig. 15}.

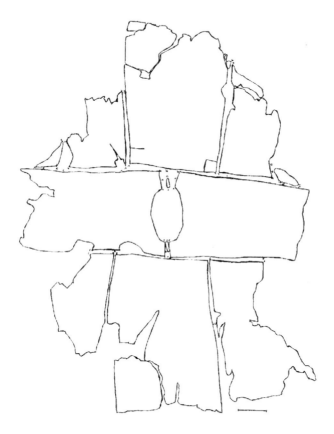

Fig. 15. Find from Møgelmose, Denmark. Sketched at the National Museum, Conservation Department, Lyngby.

Tanners in literature

The Book of Genesis 3:21 reads, "And the LORD God made for Adam and for his wife garments of skins, and clothed them;" and in Exodus 26:14 the Lord describes to Moses how the Tabernacle (desert temple) shall be made: "And you shall make for the tent a covering of tanned rams' skins and goatskins."

The status of leather-working has varied; producing parchment for holy scriptures was an honorable profession, while the social standing of the tanner could be low.

In the Jewish law which came into their present form circa 200 B.C., we can find words of wisdom such as, "The world needs both perfume-makers and tanners; happy is he who is born to be a perfume-maker, woe is he who is born to be a tanner." A woman who married a tanner "in spite of his defect" had the right to a divorce if the husband brought the smell of the tannery home with him. She merely needed to say, "I thought I could stand it, but no more" to be divorced [Babylonian Talmud; Ketuvot 77, recto]. Tanneries could not be built of lumber which had been used in a synagogue.

We can deduce that tanning had a higher status in Greece through reading the Iliad, where Homer sings of tanning with oils; "As when a man gives the hide of a great ox, a bullock, drenched first deep in fat, to all his people to stretch out; the people take it from him and stand in a circle about it and pull, and presently the moisture goes and the fat sinks in, with so many pulling..." (Iliad XVII, 389). The great Homeric epic probably existed in more or less completed form around 700 B.C. (Lagerlöf/Bendz 1958: IX). The tanner in classical Greece was seen as an extremely necessary person in as much as he produced materials for helms, shields and footwear.

It is interesting that in all written sources in which tanning is seen as a profession, it is seen as man's work; while if we go to the comparative ethnographic material we see that in the societies where hunting and fishing is a way of life, leather-working seems for the most part to have been women's work, although the men in some cases helped out with the heavier work (Barber, 1994: 29-33).

Leathercraft as an everyday task

Knowledge of how to preserve hides and leather was probably common to all people to a certain extent, so long as they lived a life in which each individual depended on being able to survive with the help of available resources. In the Swedish hunting stone age (12,000-4,000 B.C.), people were dependent on leather for protection from the cold; during the agricultural stone age (4,000-1800 B.C.) sheep, and from them, wool, gradually came into use; and from the bronze age (1800-500 B.C.) we have traces of woven cloth. Cloth was able to replace leather to a certain extent, but warm furs and sturdy leather shoes are still important even today.

In order to seek out more clues as to how the first inhabitants of Sweden preserved their leather, I have looked to the peoples who have lived and continue to live in similar circumstances.

Leathercraft as an everyday task can be found today, mostly among those peoples who to some extent still live as hunters and reindeer herders, and it was to those people that I turned and asked to partake of their knowledge.

* In Europe, the early Stone Age is divided up into three major periods: the early paleolithic (around 700,000-130,000 years ago), the mid-paleolithic (130,000-35,000 years ago), and the late paleolithic (35,000-12,000 years ago) (Sklenar 1989:4).

THE INUIT

Inuit means "people" in Inuktituk, the language of the Inuit, and is the reindeer-people's name for themselves. Eskimo is a nickname given to them by the Indians, and means "those who eat raw meat."

"The tent and the igloo are really only auxiliary shelters. The real home of the Ihalmio* is much like that of the turtle, for it is what he carries about on his back. In truth it is the only house that can enable men to survive on the merciless plains of the Barrens. It has central heating from the fat furnace of the body, its walls are insulated to a degree of perfection that we white people have not been able to surpass,or even emulate. It is complete, light in weight, easy to make and easy to keep in repair. It costs nothing, for it is a gift of the land, through the deer.... Primarily the house consists of two suits of fur, worn one over the other, and each carefully tailored to the owner's dimensions. The inner suit is worn with the hair of the hides facing inward and touching the skin while the outer suit has its hair turned out to the weather. Each suit consists of a pullover parka with hood, a pair of trousers, fur gloves and fur boots. The double motif is extended to the tips of the fingers, to the top of the head, and to the soles of the feet, where soft slippers of harehide are worn next to the skin. The high winter boots may be tied just above the knee so that they leave no entry for the cold blasts of the wind. But full ventilation is provided by the design of the parka. Both inner and outer parkas hang slackly to at least the knee, and they are not belted in winter. Cold air does not rise so that no draughts can move up under the parkas to reach the bare flesh, but the heavy, moisture -laden air from close to the body sinks through the gap between parka and trousers, and is carried away. Even in times of great physical exertion, when the Ihalmio sweats freely, he is never in danger of soaking his clothing and so inviting quick death from frost afterwards. The hides are not in contact with the body at all, but are held away by the soft resiliency of the deer hairs that line them, and in the space between the tips of the hair and the skin of the parka, there is a constantly moving layer of warm air, which absorbs all of the sweat and carries it off.... In summer the outer suit is discarded and all clothing pared down to one layer. The house then offers effective insulation against heat entry." (Mowat, 1952: 122 ff).

The basic principles for the shaping of the clothes, as well as the method of the skins' preparation, seem to some extent to be common to the peoples who live in similar climates. The cut of the clothes and of the kamik (footwear), on the other hand, varies. Different tribes have their own styles and in the past one could tell a person's tribe by his clothes. Many different animals' skins are used, e.g. reindeer, seal, polar bear, dog, fox, wolf, squirrel, bird and fish.

The Caribou-Inuit

For the most part, I will describe here what I learned from the Inuit in Arviat, a little village some 500 km (about 300 mi.) north of Churchill in Hudson Bay, Canada.

The methods used by women here to make their skins soft and comfortable to wear, or watertight for use as footwear, have probably not changed in millennia.

It is first and foremost the rein- deer's skin, or the caribou's, as the somewhat larger North American reindeer is called, which has come to be used in clothing {fig. 16}.

Reindeer skin is preferred be- cause of its ability to retain heat: each hair is hollow and filled with air; in addition, they are coarser at the top and finer down toward the root, which means that a pocket of air is created between each hair.

The Inuit take advantage of the variations in the color and length of reindeer-skin's hair. By collecting bits from different parts of the skin, coats are made with great flexibility and pretty patterns. A well-dressed hunter shows respect for the animal and thus receives greater success in the hunt {Fig. 17}.

The women's clothes are sewn with lots of room in the back, so

Fig. 16. Ragnifer tarandus.
"The Caribou got its name from the Micmac Indians in eastern Canada. The word means 'shoveler' and al- ludes to the reindeer's way of digging in the snow with its outspread hooves to find nourishment."
[Världens Djurliv, 1980: 31].

that a child can be carried next to the mother's body inside the coat; the hood is large so as to shield the mother and child from the wind and cold.

Fig. 17. Hunting costume in caribou skin, sewn by Madelaine Kringayark, Repulse Bay.

Some garments have large shoulders so that the mother can move the child forward to her breast without having to take it out into the cold. These women's clothes, made to carry a child, are called *amautik* {Fig. 18}. The clothes were once sewn with bone needles, sealskin thimbles and sinew thread, but today steel needles and thimbles are used. Sinew thread is still used, but nylon thread is becoming more and more common.

When the slain animal is flayed, the skin is cleaned of fat and spread, or, stretched out to cool and dry. Skins which have been spread out on the ground to dry are used for clothing, since they are softer after preparation than those which have been stretched out to dry.

The dried skins are taken home and the softening process begins. The leather's outermost part, the so-called grain, is made to crackle through mechanical processing. A very particular sound is made by this processing, similar to the sound of ripping cloth. Afterwards, the strands of hair can be seen sitting in small bunches, separated from one another. Then the skin is moistened and folded up to rest a few hours before the actual scraping begins, when all the membranes are removed and the skin acquires its final softness.

13

Since these skins are not actually tanned, their durability is short and the women who were my teachers, Leah Okatsiak and Elizabeth Nibgoarsi, prepared seven skins in this manner every year for every hunter in the family, in order to sew new clothing for them.

The garments often have fringes along the bottom, and when the wind hits these fringes it is broken up and doesn't blow up against the body from beneath. The fringes also act as moisture conductors, and help the garment retain its shape.

In *Nordvästpassagen* ("The Northwest Passage") we can read how the crew was equipped with Eskimo clothing: "Both anoraks and trousers are often edged with fringes. In the beginning, before the members of the expedition had become altogether used to the Eskimo clothes and taken them seriously, there were several who thought it foolish that grown men should go about with fringes on their clothes; therefore they cut them off. But I had some second thoughts about that, since I had noticed that nothing in the Eskimo's clothing or equipment in general was without purpose and meaning——and thus I let mine alone in spite of the others' jeering. But he who laughs last laughs best: and one fine day, the anoraks whose fringes had been cut began to roll up, and would soon have been useable as scarves if the fringes hadn't been replaced in a hurry." (Amundsen 1979: 167f.)

Fig. 18. Elizabeth Nibgoarsi in her amautik *of caribou skin, with the hair turned inwards.*

In warmer weather, garments of sealskin are used. Sealskin is significantly more durable and water-resistant. In this area, it is for the most part the ringed seal whose skin is prepared and sewn into anoraks, trousers,

14

gloves and kamik uppers.

The much larger bearded seal has a significantly thicker hide, which is used for watertight kamik soles {fig. 19}.

Fig. 19. Top: Ringed seal (Phoca hispida).
Bottom: Bearded seal (Erignathus barbatus).

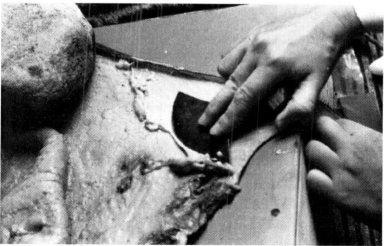

Fig. 20. Slicing away the fat on the sealskin's flesh side.

Preparation begins with the cutting away of the thick layer of blubber on the flesh side with the sharp ulo {Fig. 20}.

15

If the skin is to be dehaired, there are two ways to go about it:

1: The skin is most watertight if the hair is sliced away; the roots then remain in the follicles and the epidermis remains as a protective outer layer {Fig. 21}.

2: Warmer, but less watertight, skin can be made by soaking the skin in water for about a week or dipping it in hot water for a few seconds. The hair is then scraped off, and the roots and epidermis follow. The follicles are filled with insulating air.

After the dehairing, a thin layer of the leather itself is sliced off, making the skin more flexible; after which, the skin is stretched on a frame to dry. If the skin is to be used for soles, the sole is cut out and chewed until soft; this takes 3-4 hours per sole {Fig. 22}.

Fig. 21. Slicing off the hair.

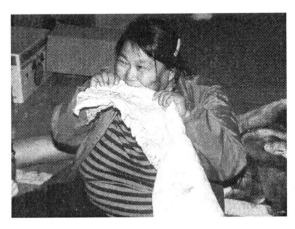

Fig. 22. Leah Okatsiak softens a reindeer skin.

16

If a man's kamik have gotten damp and stiffened during a night's drying, the women will chew them soft for him in the morning before he puts them on again. White men who use sealskin kamik usually soften their soles themselves by rubbing them over a stick, called a "white man's woman." Fur is prepared the same way, in principle, as dehaired skin, but is softened by first twisting it up into a bundle and then trampling it soft.

The first clothing

How the Inuit's clothing was created is told in the legend of the Moon Man.

"The Moon Man was a cruel man who, from his house on the moon, kept a watchful eye over the dwelling-place, making sure that all the death-related rites and instructions were followed. The Moon Man also directed the flood and ebb, and had power over people's, animals', birds' and fishes' fertility; often the shaman had to undertake a dangerous voyage in order to persuade the Moon Man to make a childless woman fertile. If the ceremonies for a death were not performed in the right way, then the Moon Man came travelling dressed as a bear from top to toe, to punish the careless one and his household with his cane, a colossal walrus-tusk. His anorak was a whole bear-skin, flayed from the slain animal in one piece after the hind legs were cut off at the shin and the front paws removed from the front legs. The opening around the maw became the hole in the hood through which the Moon Man showed his face. The skin from the front paws became gloves and the hide from the hind legs became trousers and kamik. Both in front and behind the jacket a 'tail' or tip hung down: the bear's sex organ and tail; and it is especially these 'tails' we find so prominent on the Eskimos' fur jackets. When a woman sews a fur coat, it is actually a reconstruction of a he-animal... It is not enough to recreate the animal's skin--the skeleton is also marked by setting in strips of light and dark skin, for example on the outside of the arms... The carefully and clearly marked edges around all the skin's openings show the cuts which were made when the skin was removed from the animal's body {Fig. 23}. The captured and slain animal's soul shall be appeased by the offer; if it happens correctly then the animal will come back and let itself be captured again. This presentation is also the basis for recreating the animal's exterior when, after preparation, one sews a garment. By letting the animal's skin reappear unchanged, one shows the animal the respect its soul requires, and in return the people get a part of the animal's ability to survive in the harsh environment." (Rosing 1979: 35).

Ihalmio means "small hill." This group of Inuit live in the Canadian inland and are named for the appearance of the landscape.

Fig. 23. The polar bear's skin becomes a suit. (Drawn from Rosing 1979: 35).

An idea of how the Thule-Inuit's clothing looked in the 15th century can be gotten from a find which was made in 1972 at the old winter settlement, Qilakitsoq in northern Greenland{Fig. 24.}. Five hundred years earlier, a little Inuit community here was stricken by a catastrophe; six women and two children were killed. They were buried in two graves under a projecting cliff. The dry climate, frost and wind caused the people and their clothes to be freeze-dried, and thus they were preserved until now. The clothing is made principally of sealskin, but there are also several inner coats sewn of eiderduck's breast. These were worn with the feathers against the body and are very warm and soft, but not so durable. The women's anoraks have high hoods, possibly to allow space for high coiffures; they are low-cut so that they can be drawn over the head, and many of the anoraks are cut high over the shoulders. On one of the garments, loose bits of seal-pup skin

Fig. 24.

have been tacked on, possibly to protect the shoulders from the cold. There is a saying among the Inuit which goes, "A skillful seamstress makes her spouse into a good hunter." In these clothes we have proof of the dead women's skill as seamstresses. The clothes are located in Landsmuseet in Nuuk, Greenland.

18

THE INDIANS

"The original clothing of the North Americans consisted entirely of furs and skins; one piece is fastened around the waist, another larger piece is thrown over the shoulders. Their leggings are of skin, shaped to the leg; the seams are decorated with porcupine quills. The shoes are made from deerskin, and are made to fasten around the ankles, where they have decorations of brass or tin, about an inch long, hanging from the laces. The women are covered from the knees up. Their tunics cover the body but not the arms. The skirt extends from the waist to the knees; both are of leather. Shoes and leggings are similar to the men's." [Hungry Wolf, 1971: 2, author's transl. {Hungry Wolf is quoting from John McIntosh's book, *The Origin of the north American Indians*, ca. 1840}]

As early as the time referred to above —that is, the mid-1800's—contact with the white man had begun to influence the clothing style, and the Indians began more and more to adopt the new materials which the fur-traders brought with them.

Since the Scandinavian Vikings visited Newfoundland in the 11th century, there have been sporadic contacts between Europeans and Canada's Inuit and Indians. In the 15th century, the kings of Europe began to send out adventurers to conquer and christen the new land. The English concentrated in the area around Newfoundland. The French moved up along the St. Lawrence River and founded a French colony which was given the Indian name Quebec. The French fur trade spread, and hunters paid high taxes to the governor of Quebec. Two successful fur-hunters, the Frenchmen Radisson and Groseilliers, protested against the taxes and turned instead to England. With support from King Charles II, the Hudson's Bay Company was born in 1670 and Englishmen began to set up a series of trading posts. Indians and Inuit came with furs and received goods such as flour, sugar and tobacco in exchange.

The great demand for furs in Europe depended primarily on a new fashion in hats. Large felted fur hats were popular, and hatters discovered quickly that beaver's underwool was unsurpassed as a raw material for the making of these hats {fig. 25}.

*Fig. 25. Beaver (Canadian beaver=*Castor Canadensis; *European beaver=*Castor fiber).
Above: Beaver's felt hat.

19

That it was the wool and not the skin which was desired, is reflected in the Hudson's Bay Company's motto, "*pro pelle cutem*," which from the start had the implication "the skin for the fur." Many Indians and Inuit became dependent on the wares the fur traders brought with them and were hit hard in the times when the demand for furs lessened and the traders did not come.

The Europeans who explored North America's enormous subarctic region came in contact with, among others, the Indians who are today called Northern Athapaskan; Canada's Athapaskan Indians call themselves Dene. These Indians live in an area reaching from Hudson's Bay in the east to Alaska in the west. The Indians traveled over large areas and demanded a lot from their clothing. It had to protect against cold and snow, and against insects in the summer, it had to be light to wear and allow great flexibility. In addition, it had to be made from an easily available material. The skin of the moose, North America's elk {fig. 26}, and the caribou were preferred for clothes. But other skins were also used, e.g. beaver, otter, and jackrabbit. The caribou gave warm pelts for winter use; but like the moose-skin it could also be dehaired and oil tanned.

Fig. 26. The North American moose (left), belongs to the same species as the European, but is usually larger (Alces alces). *Elk, or wapiti (right). The North American breed of red deer* (Cervus elaphus canadensis).

The Dogrib-Indians

The woman who was my foremost teacher of Indian brain tanning methods was Helen Tobie who belongs to the tribe of Dene called Dogrib. Dogribs hunted and fished between Great Bear Lake and Great Slave Lake in the Northwest Territories. Helen, who inherited her knowledge from her mother, is a skillful tanner and seamstress. She dehairs and brain tans skins of caribou and moose. She prepares beaver pelts and uses them for edgings and decorations.

The knowledge of brain tanning of skin from moose, elk and caribou is spread over the whole North American continent, but the methods differ somewhat. The principal variations are in the method of dehairing, which grease is used, and how many times the skin is smoked. To simplify the dehairing, the skin can be laid in water and soaked; the longer the skin soaks the easier it is to dehair it, but the final result is a weaker skin.Helen doesn't soak her skins at all, but rather slices off the hair with a sharp knife {fig. 27}, which means that the roots of the hair remain in the skin, an advantage if one wishes to make a skin-boat.

Fig. 27. Helen Tobie slices off the hair from a moose hide.

If one wants to make soft clothes the roots must later be scraped out, a difficult task. Helen tans her skins with a mixture of boiled brain, lard, and soap. In times past, bone marrow was used instead of lard and ash lye instead of soap. Brain tanning is combined with smoke tanning. Helen warms and smokes the skins both before and after greasing; the warmth from the fire causes the grease to penetrate into the skin and makes it easier to scrape away the remaining hair-roots. In addition, a third smoking is done as a final treatment when the skin is dry and soft. The smoke then gives the skin a pretty golden-brown color, and increases water resistance and if the skin gets wet it will not stiffen as it dries, but rather will remain soft. If the skin is not soft enough, it is tanned again with cheese and soap. This is done before the final smoking. There are also pure white brain tanned skins; these skins were warmed without smoke and freeze-dried outdoors in deep cold and sun. Beaver skin is also prepared with a mixture of brain, lard and soap. Clara Yellowknee, a woman of the Cree Indians, told me that once she didn't have any brain at hand, so she tanned her moose skin with oatmeal boiled together with soap.

Another band among the Dene bears the name Hare. The name comes from the fact that they hunted the arctic hare (*Lagomorpha arcticus*), ate its meat and used the skin for warm, light clothes and blankets. The skin was taken in the winter when the pelt was white and the skin at its strongest. The raw hide was sliced into a long thin thong, which was rolled up on a 2-3 cm (about 1 in.) thick cane and dried. These thongs were then joined together using a method similar to that used in net-making. The result was a coat which gave the appearance of having a solid surface, but was really "a bunch of holes held together by a leather thong."

Decorations

Today people usually decorate their moccasins, jackets and gloves with glass beads, but there are still women who use the old methods with porcupine quills and moose hair embroidery. The porcupine quills are taken from the backside of the dead animal, colored and flattened before they are sewn down in complicated patterns {fig. 27a}.

The moose hair is taken from the moose's backside and shoulders in the wintertime when the hair is at its longest. The hair is gathered in small bunches, colored and sewn down, often in floral patterns.

Fig. 27a. Moccasins embroidered with porcupine quills.

THE SAMI*

"Far off to the northwest in Germania, under a high cliff on the seashore, lies a cave... Near this place live the Skate-Finns, as these folk are called... Their name can be traced to the barbarian language's word for leaping. For when they leap, they can catch up with the wild animals with the help of a hooked bit of wood, which they have skillfully fashioned to resemble a bow. In their land, there is an animal not unlike a deer; from its skin, thickly covered as it was with hair, I have seen a knee-length garment like a tunic, such as the aforementioned Skate-Finns use." [Diaconus, 1971:16f] This was written in the eighth century by Paulus Diaconus, and in writing of the Skate-Finns, he seems to have the Sami in mind.

In the tunic described here, we may perhaps find the model for the fur outerwear which is, even in the 20th century, still a commonly found garment among the Sami {fig. 28}.

Earlier, in the wintertime both an outer fur with the hair side out, and an inner fur with the hair turned inward, were worn.

The finest skin for furs is gotten from calves slaughtered in late July and August. The Sami have taken to holding calf-slaughterings particularly in the middle of August. These slaughterings happened almost exclusively for the sake of the furs. Later in the fall, the hair has grown longer and the skins have become thicker and harder to prepare as a fur, because they lose their hair more easily.

Fig. 28. Sami women at Jokkmokk Market, 1991.

23

The softest and most short-haired furs of all come from small reindeer calves which have only been alive for a few days or weeks. These skins are also the weakest and are used for baby blankets. In the summer, worn and hairless fur coats were used; also frocks sewn of dehaired tanned skins.

Bark-tanning

In my search for the traditional bark-tanning process, I saw that it was primarily among the Sami that the original methods have been preserved. With the Sami, as with the Inuit and the Indians, the women are the ones who prepared the skins and sewed the clothes. Furs were prepared by cutting up and boiling the inner bark of birch, sallow or willow trees.
The skins were scraped with, for example, the S-shaped scraper {fig. 8}, and then rubbed on the flesh side with the bark and bark-bath. This process was repeated several times.

Skins which are to be made into leather are dehaired by soaking and placed in the tan bath. After a few days they are hung up and left to dry a bit before they are dyed with chewed alder bark and then thoroughly rubbed with grease, such as seal-oil, butter, drippings, or neatsfoot oil. Finally, the skins are pulled and stretched until they become soft. Naturally, the method of preparing the skins can vary, and it is said, among other things, that some women mix salt in the tanning bath, and that others chop up and add fresh juniper sprigs, to get a softer leather. The juniper sprigs also give the leather a lovely aroma and seem to stop the rotting process which began during the dehairing soak. But it is important that none of the juniper's berries get into the tan, for they cause black spots on the leather.

The generally short time in the bark-bath causes the leather not to be tanned all the way through; rather, this method can be seen as a combination of bark-tanning and oil tanning.

White leather for edgings and finer work is made through simple mechanical working.

The Sami use the term sämskat skinn (chamois leather) also for bark-tanned leather, while in standard Swedish the term means only oil tanned leather. Theories to the effect that oil tanning was the original tanning method can be found in the work of several authors.

"The original Lappish tanning method seems to have been the so-called chamois-tanning, the use of grease as a leather-making agent, although this practice, with the Lapps as with other primitive peoples where it is prevalent, such as Ostjaker [an Ugrian-speaking people from the Ob region of Siberia], Samoyeds, and Chukchi, only serves to make the hide flexible. Nowadays the Lapps rub the skins with grease after bark-tanning." [Drake 1979: 195]

It was surely from observation of the red color which penetrates and dyes the hands when one cuts a slice in the bark of the alder tree that a desire to make use of this strong dye was born and the use of bark can very easily have begun from a wish to dye one's skins, perhaps both one's own skin and one's garments. Eventually it was discovered that the bark also tans the skin and that bark-tanned skins are significantly more water-resistant than those which are merely oil tanned.

Asbjörn Nesheim, who studied the Sami leather terminology, its loan-words and historical background, theorizes that the Sami learned bark-tanning from Finnish and Nordic merchants and farmers. "In the terminology we find proof for this in words such as bark and bark-bath (bar'ko) and leather (lier'hte)." [Nesheim 1964:217] Besides reindeer-skin, the Sami have also used sheep- and goatskin for clothes, and cow-hide for shoes.

One can read more about Sami costume in Susanna Jannok Porsbo's book *Samiskt Dräktskick* ("The Sami Costume").

The Sami have in the past been called "Lapps" or "Lapplanders" in English, but in recent years the people's own name for themselves has come into general use. [Translator's note]

TANNERS

The preparation of furs and the tanning of leather for trousers, aprons, shoes and thongs, was a common skill which in certain areas, especially in the countryside, survived into the twentieth century.

From having been an everyday women's chore performed in or around the home, there emerged a competition between home-tanning and professional tanning. The first written evidence that tanning was beginning to be regarded as a profession, and consequently a man's work, come from the 14th-century city code of Visby, Sweden. Here tanners and shoemakers, among others, are named. According to the civil-economic theories of the time, artisans ought to live in cities; and in the 14th century many attempts were made to get artisans, tanners among them, to move into the cities. But this was hard to bring about in Sweden because of the great distances involved.

The guild system

By the twelfth century, the guild system had begun to develop on the continent and had spread gradually to the Nordic countries. The guild was a collection of masters in the same or closely related trades, which aimed primarily to promote the quality of the wares, work for fixed prices and settled working conditions. The word "*skrå*" ("guild," in Swedish) is Old Norse and means "prepared skin." Originally, the word referred to the parchment on which the guild's charter was written.

In Malmö, tanners got a guild of their own in 1429; the tanners were to work with furry skins, but also had the right to make chamois leather. *Karduansmakarna* (Cordovan-leather makers) who prepared finer, often dyed, leather, appear in Stockholm in the late 14th century. Shoemakers tanned their own leather, but there gradually came to be specialists in bark-tanning and these split away and formed their own professional group in the 17th century. Also in the 17th century, there appeared a special guild for chamois-makers. The chamois makers worked with oil tanning.

A negative factor, however, was the monopolization which was embodied in the mandatory guild membership, and which restrained it from free competition. For each guild decided which tests a journeyman had to complete to become a master and practice the profession himself. The requirements for Danish rug-makers in 1686 were that a candidate had to prepare an elk-hide, three buffalo-hides, two deerskins, ten goatskins, ten cow-hides, and ten calfskins. From these skins he then had to make a buff-coat, a carbine strap, a long sword-harness, two pairs of gloves and a pair of leggings. The tasks were so hard that it was nearly impossible to complete them successfully, and thus the number of masters was kept low. It was said in the 17th century, "In Sweden one can strive hard and become king, but one cannot become a chamois-maker."

26

It was easier for one who was a master's son or married to a master's daughter; one could also become a master by "keeping" a widow, which meant marrying the widow of a deceased master. There is a story in the 18th century of a "*skoflickardotter*" (a cobbler's daughter) who broke the record for "being kept" for she was married to no fewer than four shoemakers in a row. [Bertel 1949: p. 46]

In the age of the Vasa kings, attitudes became harder and those craftsmen who did not move to the cities risked being conscripted for military service. Carl IX demanded of the Parliament in 1604 that all craftsmen should move to the cities. In spite of all these pressures, the rural population was not entirely willing to give up leathercraft. In 1723, the peasantry demanded of the parliament that country people should have the right to prepare skins themselves for household use. The decision was passed in parliament in 1727, though the country folk were forbidden to travel around in the country and buy up unprepared skins, prepare them and then sell them. On the other hand, it was not forbidden to wander about and prepare skins or sew furs on farms.

The tanners of Malung

It is not certain when the first tanners began to wander out among the homesteads, prepare skins and sew furs; but we know from an archive source that it was common by the end of the 17th century. "In the lower assembly on February 20, 1684, in the Malung parish house, the parish priest Georgius Salinus complained of '...how here in the parish it is very hard to get piece-workers, for the farm-hands of the parish mostly wander out in the country, to work at leather-sewing, by which they sometimes think they can escape the rank of farm-hand; and thus the vicarage ends up being ill-tended and ill-maintained.'" [Malung 1976: 18]

No area in the nation specialized so markedly in preparation of fur skins as Malung parish. Malung lies in the coolest zone of central Sweden and the animals whose skin was used for furs had long and warm fur. Many of these wandering tanners had their farms in Malung, but wandered out in the winter season in teams of tanners to earn their winter keep. Such a team might consist of: a master-tanner, three or four tanners and a *blötpojke*, or soaking-boy. The skins they prepared were mostly sheep-, goat- and calf-skin. The treatment of the skins began long before the animals were butchered. The sheeps' wool was clipped sufficiently before butchering that it would grow out to the desired length. The farmer saw that the animals were kept dry and clean for days before butchering so as not to dirty the wool. The preparation of the pelt was done primarily in one of two ways, the so-called raw-preparation or raw-stretching, and preparation with bate. With raw-preparation, the skins had simply been dried when the tanners came to the farm. Often, the youngest boy in the tanners' team, the soaking-boy, had been sent ahead the night before to soak the dried skins in water or salt water. This was done so that the tanners could immediately begin the next day to stretch, or stake, the skins [fig. 29]. These skins were prepared with seal-oil, lanolin, or lard.

Fig. 29. Perjos Halvarsson stakes a sheepskin.

For the other method, the people of the farm had bated the skins before the tanners arrived. The bate was made of flour, salt and water. The skins lay in the bate for fourteen days to a month depending on the temperature of the bath. After bating, the skins were kept in a dry place until the tanning team arrived and performed the final stretching and softening.

Whether a skin would be bated or raw-stretched depended on which animal the skin came from as well as what it would be used for. Sheepskin for fur coats was usually bated, while skins which were used for skin rugs were often raw-stretched. Raw-stretched skins end up with whiter and finer wool and also avoid the smell of the bate, which can be rather strong. Bated skins are a little easier to stretch.

These methods are more fully described in the recipe section, raw-preparation on page 46, and bating on page 61.

In 1802 the farmers were given the freedom to employ tanners out in the parishes, and in 1864 complete freedom of commerce was established, which led to the foundation of a great many tanneries in the countryside. In the period between 1871 and 1875 there were 687 tanneries in all of Sweden. During the later half of the 19th century, there began a shift from artisanal practice of tanning to the more industrial.

Towards the end of the 19th century most of the wandering tanners began to give up their work and instead there developed in Malung a factory-based leather industry. Steam and electric power were used and new, effective extracts of tanning agents were imported. The preparation became more technically complicated and required larger and larger capital investments, which meant that the smaller tanneries had difficulty keeping up with the developments; and gradually they were shut down and replaced by a few large factories.

From the 1890's on, rubber boots began to take the place of bark-tanned leather boots, which led to a smaller demand for bark-tanned leather among the tanneries of the farm settlements. The early 1900's have been called the death-decade of tanning; in 1913 the number of tanneries had sunk to 136, and today [1991] there are about a dozen tanneries, of varying sizes.

It is heartening that the trend has begun to turn around in the past ten years, and several small newly-established tanneries have sprung up.

THE STRUCTURE OF SKIN

A mammal's skin is much more than a protective casing; it is an organ in and of itself with a number of important functions. The skin must protect the body from blows and infections, regulate the body's temperature, get rid of waste products through perspiration, build up and do away with fat, and act as a sensory organ. In spite of the superficial variation visible among the various types of animals, there are nonetheless more similarities than differences with regard to the skin's function and structure. Mammalian skin consists of three layers: an upper (epidermis), middle layer (dermis), and a lower (hypodermis). The word dermis comes from the Greek *derein*, to flay, and refers to the raw skin. During recorded history, the names of the various layers have shifted. Another name for the middle layer is *corium*, a term which has been in use for 2,000 years.

The upper layer

This thin layer which is called the epidermis can itself be divided into several layers. The outermost layer, or basal layer, consists of dead and hardened cells. The basal layer's thickness depends on what kind of usage the skin is subjected to. It is for this reason, for example, that thick calluses develop on the hands and feet. This layer is used up little by little as our skin flakes away. It grows from underneath by way of cell-division in the bottom-most layer. The cells are changed on their migration upwards and are completely hardened by the time they reach the surface.

The hair is also considered to be a formation of the epidermis. The roots of the hair sit in follicles like a knife in a sheath and penetrate more or less deeply into the dermis. The outer skin and hair are made of the protein keratin, or horn-material. Between the cell-layer and the corium, or dermis, there is a soft basement membrane. Through this layer, nutrition is transported from the corium to the outer skin. The basement membrane contains the grains of color, or pigment, that protect against ultraviolet radiation and give human skin and hair, as well as animals' pelts, their color.

The pigment grains are not completely destroyed during unhairing, which is why black- and brown-haired skins are not practical for white-tawed leather. During the unhairing process, the basement membrane is dissolved, allowing the hair and outer skin to be removed.

The middle layer

The most important part, from the tanner's point of view, is the dermis. The dermis can also be divided into two layers. The layer nearest the epidermis is called the grain-, thermostat-, or papillary layer. In this book it will be called the grain layer. When the hair and outer skin are removed the grain layer appears, with a characteristic surface appearance depending primarily on the hair follicles' number and arrangement in relation to one another. The hair follicles are embedded in the grain layer, as are the lymph ducts, tactile organs, sweat- and sebaceous glands. A muscle (the *erector pili*) goes from the grain layer down to each hair-root; in dangerous situations or in the cold this muscle contracts, which causes the hair to stand up and the pelt to become airier and warmer. The grain layer consists for the most part of two different fibrous proteins, collagen and elastin. The elastin fibers run parallel to the surface, while the orientation of the collagen fibers is around 90°. The very fine collagen fibers are woven around each other and form a nearly continuous surface, which yields the tight and relatively durable grain layer.

Leather gets a smoother and more elastic grain if the elastin fibers are loosened and partly removed before tanning. This is done by what is called puering, or bating.

The layer under the grain is called the corium and consists mainly of coarser collagen fibers which branch and wrap around one another in a three-dimensional fiber-network {fig. 30}.

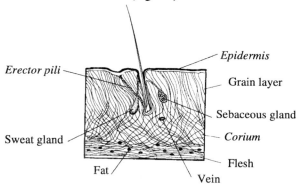

fig. 30: Skin, cross section [Thorstensen, 1969:20].

Collagen means "glue-former" and in boiling water this material dissolves into glue, a fact which has been used in tanneries insofar as their by-products have been boiled into glue and sold [see p. 101]. To avoid unintentional glue formation, a raw hide should never be exposed to temperatures above 38° C (100° F).

It is this fiber-network in the skin that determines the leather's tear resistence, compactness, and elasticity. During the tanning process it is primarily this fiber-network which is transformed. The more perpendicular the fibers are to the grain, the more compact the skin becomes. In the skin's core {fig. 31}, the orientation of the fibers is from 45° to 90° towards the grain, while in the less compact parts it is between 0° and 45°.

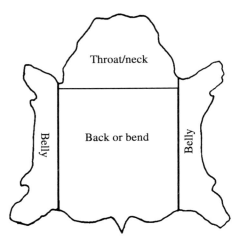

Fig. 31. Sketch of the different parts of a hide (Gustavson, 1944: 262).

The general orientation is from the head toward the tail, which gives the leather more strength in that direction, although it has greater elasticity from flank to flank. The grain layer has nearly the same thickness over the whole skin, but the thickness of the fiber-network varies significantly.

Finished leather has a smooth, even side, the grain, and a fuzzy side where the ends of the fibers--sliced off during the scraping process--can be seen, called the flesh side.

With improper handling, the skin can split at the layer where the grain merges into the fibre network layer, which can cause the grain to become wrinkled and in some cases even come loose from the layer beneath; the result then is a piece of leather which is fuzzy on both sides.

A viscous substance is found as a protective and lubricating envelope around the fibers. This ground substance, which also is found in the basement membrane, contains (among other things) undesirable proteins which would act on the leather as a cement if they were allowed to remain. Therefore, the tanner tries to dissolve out these proteins in the pre-tanning processes, such as soaking.

The under-skin

Under the dermis is the hypodermis, or connective tissue layer, with inlaid fat cells. Here also are the muscles which are used when, for example, we wrinkle our foreheads or when a horse twitches a part of his skin to get rid of irritating flies. These layers shield the proteins of the dermis from reacting with other chemicals, and must always be removed before tanning.

Protein chemistry

Collagen. To understand the chemistry of tanning, one must understand how the proteins in skin look and act, especially the two that play the main parts in the process: keratin in the epidermis and collagen in the dermis.

Proteins are nature's building blocks and are found in animals and people, in muscles and in skin. Different proteins have different structures, but are basically built from the same parts, amino acids, of which there are approximately twenty kinds. Collagen is formed when amino acids curl themselves together into long spiral-shaped chains {fig. 32 a,b}.

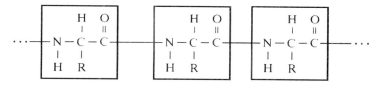

Fig. 32a: *Amino acid chain. Amino acids twist up into long chains. R represents side groups of which the most important are —NH2, the amino group, and —COOH, the carboxyl group.*

Fig. 32b: *Alpha-helix spiral. Each amino acid chain twists up into a clockwise alpha-helix spiral.*

Such a collagen chain is called an alpha-helix spiral and contains about 1,050 amino acids.

Three alpha-helix spirals twist around each other to form a triple helix spiral, which constitutes a collagen molecule {fig. 33}.

Fig. 33: Collagen molecule. The assembled collagen chains gather together three-by-three to form a collagen molecule.

Fig. 34: Fibril. Many collagen molecules join together and form fibrils that then form the actual fiber. The stripes show where the collagen molecules have bonded together.

These collagen molecules link together to form fibrils. In an electron microscope at 80,000x magnification, fibrils look like long worms whose stripes mark where the collagen molecules are bound together. Several fibrils form elementary fibers which in turn are gathered together in fiber bundles of varying thickness {fig. 35}.

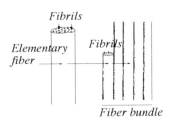

Fig. 35. Elementary fibers. Several fibrils form elementary fibers which in turn go together into fiber bundles of varying thickness.

The dermis is made up of a three-dimensional fiber network consisting of such fiber bundles. The amino acids that make up the collagen chains have chemical groups bound to them, side-groups that stick out of the fiber and and can act upon and react with their surroundings. Different amino acids have different side-groups; the most important ones in collagen are the carboxyl group —COOH and the amino group —NH_2.

The fibers in raw hide are surrounded by ground substance and water; when the hide dries and the moisture is removed, the soft fibers clump together and the hide becomes hard and stiff.

The objective of tanning is to cause various chemicals to bond to the collagen chains and form bridges between the component parts of the fibers, so that they are kept separate. This gives the fibres an open structure and makes the leather supple and pliable

The functions of the proteins depend on their three-dimensional structure; if the structure is broken up they lose their characteristics. Strong salt solutions, acids and bases can break up the bonds in proteins and cause them to change their form and character. High temperatures can also alter the structure; collagen changes to gelatin at high temperatures [see glue-boiling, p. 101]. The exact temperature at which the collagen structure breaks apart depends on whether the skin is raw or tanned, that is on how and how much tanning chemical has bonded to the collagen molecules. This is called the skin's shrinkage temperature and can provide information about how the skin is tanned {fig. 36}.

Tanning method	Shrinking temperature when heated in water	
	(°C)	(°F)
Untanned hide	58-68	135-155
Limed hide	32-50	90-122
Alum	49-63	120-145
Fat	50-65	122-150
Formaldehyde	63-78	145-172
Vegetable	70-85	158-185
Chrome	75-100	167-212

Fig. 36: Shrinking temperatures, taken from Reed, 1972: 318.

Keratin resembles collagen in structure but has one important difference. Keratin contains an amino acid whose sulfur atoms can bond to one another and form sulfur bridges between the fibers' component parts {fig. 37}, which makes keratin resistant to chemicals and hard to destroy. It is partly because of these sulfur bridges that hair stays soft even in a dry condition.

Enzymes are a type of protein that tanners have learned can help them with unhairing, puering, or bran-bating. Enzymes are found in all living material, and participate in and speed up biological processes, both constructive and destructive, without themselves being changed.

Enzymes are dependent both on pH level and temperature. Most function best at a nearly neutral pH and a temperature around 34-40° C (about 85-105° F). Boiling destroys enzymes and causes them to lose their activity.

pH value, that is the degree of acidity or alkalinity, is a measure of the concentration of hydrogen ions in a solution. On a logarithmic scale, pH values lie between 0 and 14. Solutions with a pH value of 7, for example, chemically pure water, are called neutral, while those with a pH lower than 7 are acidic. The lower the pH value, the more acidic the solution. A pH value higher than 7 indicates that the solution is basic, or alkaline.

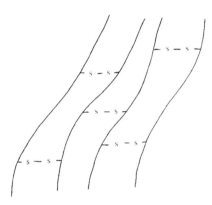

Fig. 37: Keratin contains sulfur which binds together the fibers' component parts with sulfur bridges.

Fig. 62 (see p. 67). Aldehydes react with the amino groups on the collagen chains.

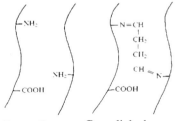

Free collagen chains   Cross-linked collagen chains

HIDES AND SKINS

The distinction between hides and skins is in their size. Hides come from larger animals, for example, ox, bull, cow, horse, elk and reindeer. Skins are taken from, calf, goat, sheep, pig and hare, etc. The term skin is also used to describe a dressed furskin. It is common to use the word tanning when the fur is removed and the word dressing when the fur is retained. Here, the words hides and tanning are used as generic terms when there is no need to specify either one or the other of these distinctions.

When one works with tanning and dressing, one realizes quickly the extent to which the quality of the raw material affects the final result. The animal's breed, sex, age, and so forth are factors which influence the choice of tanning method and the result. Diet and climatic conditions have an influence on the hide's quality. Animals that live in the open and in mountainous areas have a tighter and smoother hide than stall animals. The hide's thickness varies with the seasons, so that it becomes stronger in the winter. The age of the animal also plays an important role. As a rule, younger animals leave hides with a finer structure, but they are also thinner and weaker. Animals with thick fur often have thinner hides. Sick animals produce bad hides. Animals that have died of natural causes can be recognized in that the flesh side is red when it is fresh, even when it has been freed of blood and flesh; blue spots can also appear. Healthy hides are white.

In this section, I will offer suggestions as to how I prefer to tan various animals' hides and skins. The methods named are more thoroughly described in the recipe section which follows.

Cattle

Most cowhides, including the Scandinavian ones, produce a tight and durable hide and lend themselves wonderfully to vegetable tanning for leather. The hide's structure, its tightness and thickness are very different in cow-and bull-hides. Most highly valued are the calf-skins, and highest of all are cow-calf skins. Somewhat older heifer-hides are also very good as raw material; while older, much-milked cows are significantly worse. The most valuable part of the hide, the core section, is situated along the back from the neck to the tail and along the sides towards the middle of the belly. The core section of the heifer-hide is compact and diminishes gradually towards the belly and throat. Bull-hide has a relatively thin core section, while the belly and throat are thick but porous. Ox-hide is more like heifer-hide, but thicker and tighter. The thicker bull and ox hides are used, among other things, for sole leather and straps. The thinner calf-, heifer-, and cow-skins can be used for uppers, handbags, bellows, sandals, etc.

Cattle hides can also be dressed as furs, most simply with alum, and be used for rugs. The thin suckling-calf skins with tight and even hair-growth make fine furs. These are dressed with either alum or oil.

Horse

Horse hides have not been used to any great extent. Horse hide is quite variable in thickness and tightness. Symmetrically around the base of the tail is the so-called shell, where the hide consists of tightly interwoven fibers that make it unusually compact. The throat and belly, on the other hand, are thin and spongy. From the shell a vegetable tanned leather has been produced, which has been used as shoe uppers, blacksmith aprons, and for insoles. As chrome-tanning gained ground, people began to make the front portion into a soft and elastic upper, the so-called horse-kid.

Moose

Moose skin is more porous than cattle-skins and has a softer grain. As a result, people have most often chosen to remove the grain and oil tan the hides, which results in chamois leather. A large bull moose hide can be thick and difficult to tan, while cows and the younger animals more easily give a fine and soft skin, suitable for clothes. Trousers and vests of chamois have been quite common in Sweden all the way up to the 1900's. Moose hide can also be bark-tanned, but it doesn't become particularly waterproof or durable. The thickness of elk-hide varies with the season, The Indian woman, Mary Commanda, says that "[t]he moose hide starts getting thicker from June to December. After December it starts to get thin again. We like to get moose hide in the spring when it's easier to tan." [Gidmark, 1980: p. 28] Oil tanning of moose skin is the technique which survived primarily among the Indians of North America. The chamois leather is used for moccasins and jackets. Moose has not been used much for fur-skins, probably because [being hollow] the hairs are easily broken. The only use I know of is that the short-haired shanks, the leg-skins, are prepared in a bark-bath and used in footwear.

Deer

Deerskin has approximately the same area of use as elk-skin; however, it is considered to be somewhat stronger. It gives fine chamois leather as well as bark- or alum-tawed leather. According to Mary Commanda, "[d]eer hide gets thicker in the fall too, but in the spring it's thin as paper. So we look for deer hide in the fall." [Gidberg 1980: p. 28] If the animal is taken early in the fall, one can also get a fine fur-skin. The fur is dressed with a tan bath or alum paste. The most common deer in Sweden are red deer and fallow deer.

Roe-deer

Small, with relatively thin skins, they have usually been chamois tanned but can also be bark tanned or alum-tawed. Skins which are to be prepared as furs should be shot early in the fall; later in the year they are subject to rotting and will lose their hair as a result. Furs are dressed with a tan bath or alum paste.

Reindeer

Historically, reindeer skin was used primarily for furs. Each strand of hair is hollow and conical; the air in the hair-strands and in the pocket formed between each strand acts as insulation and makes reindeer-skin the warmest of the furs. When the skin gets wet, the water is sucked down into the hair-roots, so the surface of the pelt always feels dry.

However, as a fur its durability is short; the skin is subject to rotting which leads to hair loss. The animals slaughtered in August and September yield tighter-haired skins than those slaughtered late in the fall or the winter.

The skin from the shanks and on the pate are significantly tighter-haired than the rest and are most often used for shoes and footwear. Furs can be dressed with alum paste or tan bath.

Reindeer also yield a pretty and durable leather; the softest is the skin which comes from old females. A scourge that the Scandinavian reindeer shares with the North American caribou is the grub/warble fly; *Hypodermis bovis*. In summer the flies lay their eggs in the reindeer's hair, the larvae hatch and burrow through the skin. The larvae then develop in growing boils, until they crawl out through the skin and leave small holes behind. These holes heal during the fall and winter, and can only be seen as small scars. Thus, it is a good idea to take skins that will be unhaired at the winter slaughter. Old, worn-out, untanned bed-skins can be unhaired and tanned, and then yield a soft leather. The skins can be chamois-tanned, but I prefer to keep the pretty grain and bark tan them. Alum tawing also works well.

Sheep

Sheep-skins have a loose structure and contain a quantity of fat cells whose function is to lubricate the wool. The skin along the back and in the neck area contains much fat. A large number of fat glands in the layer where the grain merges into the dermis reduces the skin's worth for leather preparation and leads to a risk that a mis-prepared skin can separate into two parts. The grain layer in sheep, as in goat, is approximately equal in thickness to the dermis, as compared with ox-hides where the grain layer makes up only 1/6 of the dermis. There are many breeds of sheep, and the quality of their skins varies. Generally, the Nordic native breed is considered to give a relatively good leather. The skins were usually chamois-tanned or alum-tawed, but can also be bark tanned. The lamb's skin, which is more valuable than the grown sheep's, has been glacé-tanned, and used for gloves.

The sheepskin is as a rule worse, the longer and better the wool is. This is because the holes from the many wool fibers and hair follicles leave an open and loose skin behind them.

Sheepskin is most important as a fur-skin. The most important breed in our country is the aforementioned native breed, which can be divided into pelt, rug, and fine-wool sheep. Important to the choice of a fur-skin is that the wool be free from too much chaff and other foreign objects.

A fur contaminated with urine becomes yellowish even after washing. Large, long-haired skins are heavy and difficult to prepare. Sheep which are sheared about a month before slaughter give a fine, short-haired wool. These skins are most easily dressed with fat or alum.

More on the various breeds of sheep can be found in the book *ULL [Wool]*, by Kerstin Gustafsson and Alan Waller, from LTs förlag.

Goat

Goatskin is, in the sense of tanning technique, more valuable than sheepskin; it has a much tighter structure and is also more durable. It gives a very pretty bark-tanned leather as well as a fine chamois leather. Kidskin gives a fine glacé-leather and has historically been used for gloves. Kidskin also lends itself well to being dressed as a fur, with fat or alum for example.

Pig

Pig skins have a unique structure; they are extremely fatty and relatively thin. The hairs pierce straight through the skin and leave small holes behind when they are removed, which makes the skin porous and airy. The greater part of the fat sits under the dermis, however, which means that the fiber structure is not too loose; and vegetable-tanned skins can give a fine leather. A thicker and stronger leather is produced from boars than from tame pigs. The flesh side is covered with a thick layer of fat and the hair-roots penetrate through, which causes them to be broken when the flesh side is scraped, at which point the hairs fall out.

Beaver

Beavers have a soft under-wool, which is protected by stronger surface hairs. Historically, felted beaver was common -- that is, the guard hairs were pulled loose and the skin was left with only the soft under-wool. Beaver skin contains much fat and therefore it is important that the flesh side be scraped thoroughly clean before the skin is dried or salted. A dried yellowed beaver-skin is next to impossible to dress.

The simplest method for dressing beaver-skin is with an alum bath; another variant is to lay the skin in urine overnight and then work in the fat in the course of the softening process. The skin of the beaver is difficult to work and hard to get soft. But the pretty fur makes it well worth the effort.

40

Badger

Badger has a coarse, brush-like, grey-white and black pelt. The hairs usually are deep and sometimes stick out on the underside. Always scrape a badger-skin from the back to the front so as to avoid breaking the hair-roots. The fur is most easily dressed with alum. The skin is watertight and durable.

Seal

The smaller breeds of seal, such as the ringed seal (*Phoca hispida*), were usually dressed with the hair remaining. Among the local peoples, no direct tanning was used; but if one wants to use the skins in our climate, I recommend a fat or alum preparation. Larger seals such as the bearded seal (*Erignathus barbatus*), with thicker hide, were unhaired and used in footwear, untanned, by local peoples. If one wants to make leather from sealskin, I suggest vegetable tanning. Sealskin is watertight and durable.

Hare

The most common hare in Sweden is the woods hare (*Lepus timidus*). The skins are very thin, but the fur is warm and soft. The winter pelt is white in the north, but greyer farther south. Only hares shot in the winter are worth dressing. They are prepared in an alum bath.

Rabbit

There are many different breeds with different qualities. Generally speaking, rabbits have somewhat stronger skins than hares. The skins can successfully be dressed in an alum bath, but not the larger breeds; skins can also be unhaired and alum-tawed, oil, or bark tanned.

Marten, mink and fox

Marten, mink and fox are skins that are hunted in the winter time for their pelts. Wild skins that have a blue-black tone on the flesh side are not full-pelted, which means that the winter pelt has not fully grown out. The hairs do not sit as well and the skin is thinner; the blue color shows the deep-set, blood-filled hair follicles. A full-pelted skin has a white flesh side. It is easiest to dress the skins in an alum bath, but preparation with fat can also work well.

Squirrel

For the skin to be of good quality, the hunt must occur in the winter time; preferably in the early winter when the squirrel has gotten its long grey winter pelt, whence the name "grey-work". The further north one goes in Sweden, the prettier the skins are. Squirrel skin has been of great importance in the areas where taxes could not be paid in farm or livestock products. The so-called skin tax was often paid in grey-work.

We can see that squirrel-hunting was important from the district seal of Jämtland which dates from the beginning of the fourteenth century, which includes two hunters shooting squirrels in trees {fig. 38}. Squirrel skin is dressed in an alum bath.

Fig. 38: Jämtland's district seal from the beginning of the fourteenth century [Malung: p. 36].

Fish

Fish-skin has a completely different structure from mammalian skin. The scales sit loosely in pockets and the grain has an appearance similar to a bees' honeycomb {fig. 39}. The most commonly used skins come from eel, shark, catfish, burbot and salmon. Fish with scales should be scaled. The skins were usually used after being dried and softened, or prepared with urine. The skins were used for straps, bindings, shoes and clothes.

Fig. 39. Fishskin; enlarged to show grain.

Bird

Pelts of bird-skin have appeared in arctic regions. These pelts are light and warm, but not particularly durable The birds were primarily eider-ducks and divers. The skins were not tanned, merely freed of fat by scraping or by sucking out the fat by mouth. Washing in urine and softening with pumice have also been known.

CURING

It is very important that the hide be treated correctly, directly after slaughter, so that a good result can be achieved. As soon as the animal is dead, the body's own enzyme systems begin the breakdown process, called autolysis. These enzymes are most effective at body temperature, and autolysis can be stopped by flaying the animal and letting the skin cool down. Even if autolysis can be successfully stopped, the hide is then quickly attacked from outside by microorganisms. If one cannot begin working with the hide within about two hours after slaughter, then it must be preserved. Hides which are carelessly flayed should be scraped free of flesh and fat before curing. Rinse off blood and dirt as well. Three ways to cure hides are drying, salting, and freezing.

Drying takes away the water in the hide, so that the microorganisms cannot flourish; salting draws out the water and creates an unfriendly environment which the organisms cannot use and break down into food; freezing slows the breaking-down processes, though they are not completely halted; several years in the freezer can destroy a hide.

Drying
The hide is stretched out and dried in an airy, shadowy and dry place. It can be nailed up in a frame or stretched out with loose poles. The poles are fastened to the flesh side with the help of small holes in the edges of the hide [fig. 38]. If the skin is nailed against a wall, then turn the flesh side out but try also to have an air space between the wall and the skin.

Fig. 38. Hide stretched out with sticks.

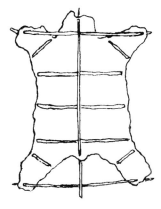

If the skin is dried in a shadowy warm climate where the drying goes quickly, the dermis is not affected much. On the other hand, if the drying goes slowly or in direct sunlight, there is almost always some sort of change in the dermis which can be difficult to discover so long as the hide is dry. During the first interval in direct sunlight, there is little damage because the the evaporating moisture keeps the temperature down; but after some time a hard surface forms which prevents the remaining moisture from evaporating, and within the hide the anaerobic (not

43

oxygen-dependent) bacteria begin to break down the hide. The risk that this will happen is greatest when drying thick hides. Flesh and fat on hides which are to be dried cause the drying to proceed too slowly. There is a risk that the hide will turn sour, or that the fat will be burned up. The hide will then become brittle and hard to scrape clean on the flesh side. Do not try to fold a dried skin, for it can break. Dried skins should be kept dry and cool. It can be useful to take a little salt in water, 1 dl salt (3.38 oz.) per 10 liters water; when dried skins are to be dressed as furs wet them down, so as to avoid the risk of hair loss.

Salting
Dry salting. Spread out the hide with the flesh side up, sprinkle it with a layer of coarse salt which will suck up the remaining blood and dirty water from the hide. Shake or brush away the salt after a day and sprinkle with new salt. Be sure the hide is covered with salt. About 10% of the hide's weight in salt is needed for the first salting, and about 40% for the second. After one or two days, the hide can be folded up with the fur side out, or if there are many hides, stacked on one another. Hides which are to be dressed as furs should be stacked with the flesh sides together. The hides should be kept dry and cool, in a cardboard box or paper bag but never in a plastic bag.

It is all right if the temperature goes below freezing, but they must not be exposed to moisture. The hides can be kept this way for up to a year, but after about six months they should be re-salted. If the hide has been salted too long, hard white salt patches form and the hide becomes brittle. Coarse salt should be used for salting. Sea salt can be used, although rock salt is preferable because its irregular grain sizes allow it to cover the surface of the hide better.

Wet salting. Hides which are bought from abroad and are to be transported long distances are usually wet salted. Immediately after slaughter, the hides are rinsed clean of dirt and blood. After they cool, the hides are prepared for a day in a 25% solution of table salt, after which they are drained and rubbed with clean dry salt. It is easier to scrape the flesh side of hides that have been salted for several weeks. Fully tanned hides that have been salted can more easily become damp, because salt remains in the hide and attracts moisture.

Freezing
Hides can also be kept frozen. If the hide is to be unhaired, it can be useful to do this before freezing; then the hide takes up less space. The whole animal can also be frozen, but it is harder to flay an animal that has been frozen. Animals that have been frozen for about a year become very hard to flay because of freezer burn. There is a risk that hides which are to be dressed as furs will begin to lose their hair while thawing. To avoid this, one can thaw the hide in salted water, 1 dl salt per 10 liters water.

44

From Norway I have heard the term *Norrlandsbark*, "Norrland bark," which meant that freezing of the hides was an integral step in the tanning process. When the water in the hide freezes, it expands and subjects the skin fibers to an internal mechanical influence which makes for softer leather as an end product.

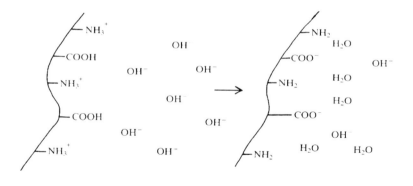

Fig. 62b (see p. 68). Collagen chains: amino groups in an acidic environment (left) and in a basic environment (right).

FLESHING

The membranes and fatty tissues that are found on the flesh side of the skin must be removed to make it possible for the tanning agents to penetrate. This is accomplished by scraping, which can also be called fleshing or scudding.

Scraping is often done in several different stages; for example, before and after dehairing, between two tanning baths, and as a final cleansing stage at the end. Final scraping is also known as perching.

If the hide is to be dehaired, one gets a smoother and better result if it is first scraped clean of remaining fat and thick membranes.

There are four different ways of scraping skins: on a scraping rack, in a stretching frame, on a beam or on a scraping post. Hides that are to be scraped on a frame, beam or scraping post, must first have their original moisture restored to them.

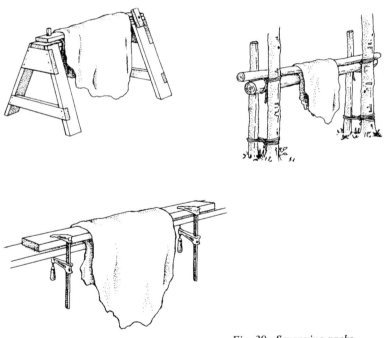

Fig. 39. Scrapping racks.

Scraping on a rack

The hide is clamped tight in a scraping rack and scraped with a scraping-spade or skin-scraper. This method is most appropriate for thinner skins such as sheep, goat, reindeer, etc. Scraping is easiest when the skin has a certain degree of moisture; if the scraper keeps slipping then the skin is too moist, if the skin gets holes in it then it is too dry.

If the skin has been salted, the salt helps provide purchase for the scraper. Flour, chalk or hardwood sawdust can be sprinkled on the flesh side now and then while scraping to dry the hide and give the scraper more purchase. Dried skins must be re-moistened before scraping. The skins are moistened with a wet rag, folded up with the flesh sides in and left overnight or until they feel moistened all the way through. A plant sprayer full of water can be handy for moistening the drier parts of a hide while scraping.

You can build a scraping rack yourself or make a temporary one with a table, a board and two clamps. You can also make one between two trees standing about 120-200 cm (about 50-80 inches) apart. The rack should be heavy and stand firm. Its height can vary between about 100 and 130 cm (about 40 and 50 inches) depending on the person's height. {See figs. 39, p. 46}.

The stake has an iron blade with a cupped handle. The shape and sharpness of the blade can vary, as can the length of the handle {figs. 40a, b, below}.

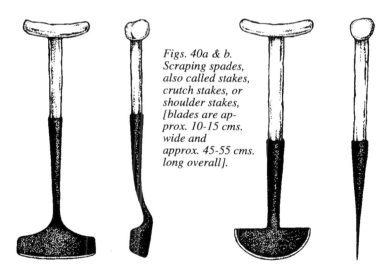

Figs. 40a & b. Scraping spades, also called stakes, crutch stakes, or shoulder stakes, [blades are approx. 10-15 cms. wide and approx. 45-55 cms. long overall].

47

I prefer to have two stakes, one sharper for scraping moist skins with lots of membrane, and one duller to stretch and soften the skins. The handle is made of wood and ends with an arched wooden block which is covered with a soft material. The blade and handle are not riveted together, but can be twisted as desired. Stand with feet apart and rest the upper body weight on the stake handle, whose cross-piece is propped against the shoulder, or into the armpit. With arm bent, work downwards from the top{fig. 41}.

Fig. 41. Working with the shoulder stake.

Always begin by scraping the edges of the skin. If the skin is scraped in the middle first, the stretch it develops in the process has no place to go, and a wrinkle forms. The book about the Malung tanners describes how this kind of scraping goes on: "The skin is stretched tight in the scraping-rack lengthwise, that is, longest along the back. About a decimeter (4 inches) from the hind leg the scraping began, and continued then forward towards the foreleg. When that was done, the skin was turned a half-turn and the other side of the skin was scraped. The edges and the leg pieces were thus scraped first. That was called 'selvaging' the skin. It was important that this was done as the first part of the scraping, so that the skin would yield during the next stage, when the skin was turned throat downwards and that part was scraped. It was said that one should 'scrape down over the throat'. If the edges had not been selvaged, then they would not yield and a wrinkle would then form in the skin, which would mean that the spade could easily slice through it. After the throat, the skin's backside was turned forward and the last stage was to scrape down to the backside." [Malung, 1976: 176f].

Be careful when scraping at first, since it is rather taxing on the muscles. The skin-scraper is good to use when the scraping-spade seems like too much work. The skin scraper has an iron blade and a wooden shaft. Hardware stores carry small paint-scrapers which can be sharpened and used as skin-scrapers {fig. 42}. At first, it is a good idea to use tools that are not particularly sharp.

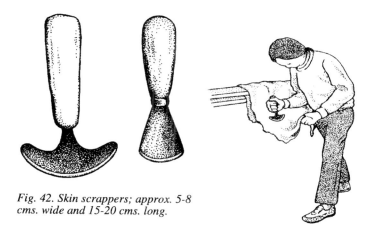

Fig. 42. Skin scrappers; approx. 5-8 cms. wide and 15-20 cms. long.

Scraping in a frame

For bigger skins, such as moose, it is often easier to stretch the skin in a frame and scrape with a bone or iron scraper. The frame is nailed together from four strong boards, about 75 x 100 mm (3 x 4 inches) If weaker lumber is used, then strengthen the corners with a cross-brace [fig. 43].

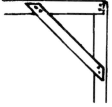

The frame should be made twice the size of the hide, which stretches a lot when it is tightened. Cut longitudinal holes around the hide about 20 mm (1 inch) from the edge, 100-150 mm (4-6 inches) apart. The hide is stretched out in the frame with rope, about 6 mm (1/4 inch); thinner rope can tear the hide. Use several short ropes instead of one long one. It is easier to center the hide in the frame if all the holes are threaded before the rope is tightened. For really *Fig. 43. Corner brace.* large hides, it can be useful to have an extra movable board to sit on, as well as a cloth to cover the sticky flesh side {fig. 44}.

A bone scraper is most useful for thicker hides which can stand up to powerful work. It is made from the metatarsal bone of, for example, moose, cow or reindeer. The bone is sawn at an angle (a hacksaw is best for this), and notched along its cutting edge. A leather band around the wrist gives extra support and power. The scraper is drawn powerfully downward, in towards the hide so as to get underneath the membranes. This scraper is used on the flesh side when the skin is relatively moist {fig. 45}.

An iron scraper is best made from the combination paint scrapers/wire brushes found in hardware stores. The paint scraper is removed and given a new handle made from a heavier type of wood, such as birch. The blade is re-sharpened and given a rounded form on its top side. This scraper is used when the skin is relatively dry {fig. 46}. When making chamois-leather, the same scraper is used on the hair side.

Fig. 44. Scraping the flesh side.

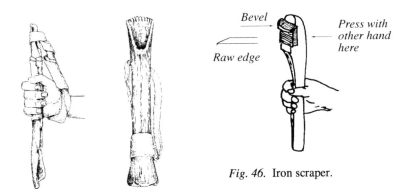

Fig. 46. Iron scraper.

Fig. 45. Bone scraper made from an elk's metatarsal bone (Mason, 1891, plate XC); see also: Fig. 45a, p. 96.

50

The tanner's beam

The beam is used mostly for thicker hides such as, for example, cowhides; it has also been used on thinner skins but these have usually been limed and thus swelled up. When working with thin skins and sharp tools on the beam, one must be extremely careful. Hides should be fully soaked when working on the beam.

The beam is made from a split post or from several boards that are joined together and given a half-round top side {fig. 47}.

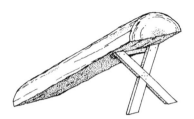

Fig. 47. Tanner's beam.

The shaving knife{[fig. 48} is used on the flesh side after soaking to skive holes in the film which formed during processing, and after de-hairing to scrape the flesh side clean. In the late 19th century, the sharp and flexible fleshing knife came to be used to scrape the flesh side of dehaired hides clean {fig. 49}.

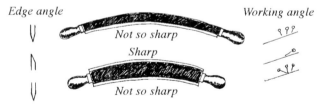

Fig. 48. Fleshing knife & combined fleshing/shaving knife.

Fig. 49. Flexible fleshing knife.

51

At the same time, the beam began to be covered with a plate of zinc so as to have a completely smooth bottom surface. The reason zinc was chosen was so that, if one were to slice down into the beam with the knife, it would not lose its sharpness. One end of the beam rests on a movable cross-brace, and the other on the ground. The hide is pressed tight between the beam's edge and the tanner's stomach. Often, several hides are laid one over the other to get a slightly yielding under-layer and decrease the risk of slicing the hide to pieces. I have used a camper's groundpad for an under-layer, and that has worked well. The various knives were adapted to the curvature of the beam.

For all work on the beam, one begins by laying the hide's tail end uppermost, towards the tanner. One begins to work in the middle as near the tail as possible and works down towards the head, then turns the hide either to the right or to the left, until one has worked all the way around the hide {fig. 50}.

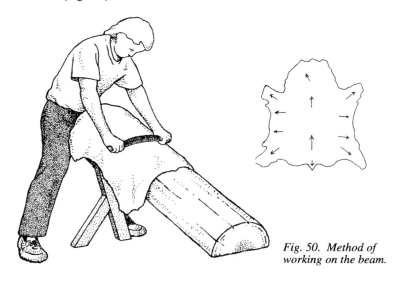

Fig. 50. Method of working on the beam.

The scraping post

Skins from small game, which are often cased, can be simpler to work on a scraping post. The post consists of a round wooden pole with a conical top {fig. 51}. The post's diameter can be adapted to the size of the skins. The skin is threaded over the post and fastened at the nose and the bottom with tacks or thumb-tacks. I prefer to sit on a chair, lean the post's end against the floor and scrape the flesh side with a small fleshing knife made from an old power hacksaw or industrial bandsaw blade {fig. 52} or a skin-scraper{fig. 42, p. 49}.

52

Fig. 51: Scraping post.   *Fig. 52: Scraping on the post.*

Begin by kneading the flesh side with hardwood sawdust, to absorb the fat that could otherwise soil the fur. Be sure the tail is split down to the end, the lips split, and the nose and ears brushed out.

The reason small game is often cased is that the furrier can then choose to cut up the skin at the sides and get a back piece and a belly piece. This way, he can sew furs with the most uniform possible hair quality.

PRE-TANNING PROCESSES

Soaking

Hides that are to be dehaired are always soaked. The primary goal is to return the hide's natural moisture level and facilitate the tanning that will follow. At the same time as the hide is moistened, it is also freed from dirt, blood, unwanted proteins and salts. Soak the hide in water, fur upwards, changing the water often if you cannot put the hide in running water. This soaking takes a varying amount of time depending on the hide's thickness and the water's temperature; the water should be soft. The following times can be used as a rule of thumb:

> Salted hides 2-4 days
> Dried hides 3-8 days.

Spots that are dried too hard and cannot be softened up, will not be able to absorb the tanning agents.

Hides that are to be prepared as fur must be soaked very carefully so as to avoid hair loss. Small game skins that are to be fur-tanned can be soaked in salt water, 1 dl salt per 10 liters water (i.e., a 1% solution by volume). Larger furs, from sheep and reindeer for example, are best soaked simply by moistening them on the flesh side with water or, if one wants to be extra careful, with salt water.

It is hard to say when people deliberately began dehairing their hides, but it must not have taken long to learn to take advantage of the fact that hair falls out under certain conditions. Among the oldest traces we have of dehaired leather are vessels made from dehaired rawhide.

If a raw hide is heated to about 65° C (150° F) in water, there is a change in the hide's proteins; the spiral-shaped collagen chains break up; the skin shrinks and becomes tacky. This property has been used to shape the hide, by fitting it to a mold and filling it with sand for example, and then exposing it to heat. People have made, among other things, hard, durable vessels this way {fig. 53}.

Many other methods have been used to dehair hides. Among them are:

> Sweating—see pp. 57-8
> Ashes—see p. 58
> Lime—see p. 58-60

Scalding. If the hide is dipped in hot water, about 70° C (160° F), for about a minute, the epidermis softens up and the hair can be rubbed off. I have only seen this method used on sealskin. It is probably the short immersion time and the fat in the skin that keep the hot water from having much effect on the dermis.

Urine. When urine is allowed to stand, it forms ammonia which removes hair due to its's alkalinity.

Mechanically. By cutting off the hair.

Fig. 53. Leather kumiss-vessels from Kazakhstan. Peter the Great Museum of Anthropology and Ethnology, St. Petersburg.

Dehairing

Dehairing should not begin before the hair comes off easily over the entire hide. Test especially at the neck and on the legs, where the hair usually is slowest to loosen. It is important to watch out for the grain; if one is too energetic at dehairing, there will be holes in the grain and the surface will appear fuzzy. When making chamois leather, the grain is scraped off to reveal this fuzzy surface.

The whole hide should be dehaired at the same time. If only parts are dehaired, they will break down more easily while waiting for the rest of the hair to loosen.

It is easiest to dehair the skins on a beam {fig. 54}. An ordinary split log smoothed off works very well. Make sure that there are no sharp splinters which can harm the hide.

Be careful to remove all of the epidermis. Left over epidermis lies like a membrane of fat over the grain, and leaves white, untanned spots in vegetable tanning. On alum-tawed leather, the epidermis appears as dull spots.

In tanneries, either an iron hair-knife with an even clean edge (notches in the edge would harm the grain), or a slate-knife was used {fig. 55}. The slate knife was used at various points in the process to press out all the waste products from the hide.

The scudding iron was a knife whose edge was first honed sharp but then smoothed with a whetstone perpendicular to the edge before it was used {fig. 56}. The scudding knife was used on the grain side to remove remaining epidermis and bits of hair. The dehaired hide was rinsed and then laid out on the beam again and stroked with one of the above named tools on both sides to press out any remaining dirt and hair-roots.

55

Fig. 54: Håkan dehairs a reindeer skin.

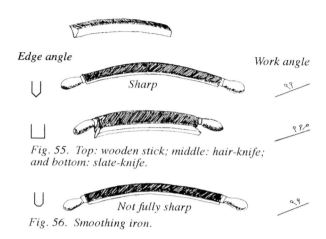

Edge angle　　　　　　　　　　　　　*Work angle*

Sharp

Fig. 55. *Top: wooden stick; middle: hair-knife; and bottom: slate-knife.*

Not fully sharp

Fig. 56. *Smoothing iron.*

Sweating

Sweating, also called putrefaction, is probably the oldest dehairing method. One deliberately initiates a rotting process. Bacteria attack the epidermis' mucus layer, which causes the epidermis and hair to loosen. The primary factors that influence the putrefaction are temperature and moisture. The rotting process goes slower at lower temperatures or if the hide is dry.

a) Lay the hide, fur upwards, in running water. Some hides, such as reindeer-hide, float and must simply be anchored to a pole with rope. It is a little more difficult with, for example, sheepskin, which sinks. Tie the skin up so that it does not lie on the bottom. Depending on the water temperature, it can take between a week and a month before the hair comes off.

b) Hides can also be dehaired under the snow. There should be about 30 cm (12 inches) of snow which is trodden down into a smooth bottom layer. Lay out the wet hide with the fur downward. Put at least as much snow on top of the hide and tread it down. You can even pour a couple of buckets of water over the assembly.

It is important that no air bubbles form between the hide and the snow. The hides usually need to lie under the snow for a couple of months. If the hair is not loose when the snow begins to thaw, one must then continue with one of the other dehairing methods.

c) A quicker way to dehair hides is in a plastic bag or bowl. The moistened hides are spread with a thin layer of soap on the flesh side—the so-called soap method. Liquid soap can be used straight out of the bottle, while solid soap should be mixed with a little water. The alkaline environment accelerates the rotting process. Fold up the hide with the hair side out and lay it in a plastic bag or covered bowl. Refold the hide once a day for the first 2-3 days and let in a little oxygen. According to the essay "Leather-working and its history," it is first the aerobic, or oxygen-dependent, bacteria which are influential, but they then give way to the anaerobic, or non-oxygen-dependent, ones [Ehrnberg, 1924: 22]. Moisten with soapy water if the hide feels dry. Then check every day how the process is progressing, by tugging at the hairs, which should come out easily. The method takes 5-10 days, depending on the temperature and the thickness of the hide. It smells bad. The bacteria can cause infection, so use rubber gloves while dehairing and be careful if you have cuts or sores on your hands. Rinse the hide thoroughly after dehairing, preferably with a little fresh soap in the rinsewater.

Ashes

We read about ashes as a dehairing agent among the Sami and Native Americans; the resulting skins are said to be extra strong. A lye is boiled from about one part hardwood ash to one part water. The ash should sink to the bottom and the clear lye is used. It should be strong enough to float a thin slice of raw potato. The lye, which is a strong base, breaks down the proteins in the mucous layer between the epidermis and the dermis. The softened skin is laid in it and left until the hairs fall out. It takes about the same amount of time as the soap method.

Another method is to sprinkle hardwood ash directly over the flesh side of the wet hide, fold it up and let it sit until the hairs fall out. When ashes are used for dehairing, the hide swells a lot, and there is a certain risk that the hides might swell so much that it becomes difficult to get the hair-roots out. After dehairing, the hides should be rinsed thoroughly in water, preferably for a couple of days.

Lime

The dehairing method which has recently been the most common is liming. The earliest reference to its use in skin processing for leather and parchment manufacture is the Lucca manuscript of ca. 800 AD (Reed, 1972: 52).

For the ancient liming method, called white liming, a super-saturated solution of slaked lime (calcium hydroxide) was used.

In the late nineteenth century, people began to add other chemicals to accelerate the dehairing processes, especially sodium sulfide, chemically represented as Na_2S. The usefulness of sodium sulfide in particular was discovered in England, when lime that had first been used as a filter in the production of gas was used for dehairing, so-called gaslime. It turned out that this lime, which contained sulfides, shortened the dehairing times (Reed 1972: 84). A certain resistance to the addition of chemicals developed, however, since the hair was usually destroyed. Hair was at that time an important byproduct which was recovered, washed and used.

Lime is extremely basic and affects the hide in several ways: it loosens up the proteins in the hypodermis so that it can be separated from the epidermis; it swells the hide and makes it more porous and more receptive to the tanning agents; it relaxes the fibers of the hide and dissolves out all unwanted fats and proteins.

Limed hides become soft and elastic. Sole-leather, for example, which should be tight and firm, would be dehaired with an acid bath, while the upper-leather would be dehaired with lime so that it would be supple.

Mix about 30-40 grams of slaked lime per liter of water (about 40-50 ounces per gallon). Lime dissolves in water up to a concentration of about 0.16% (16 grams per liter of water, or about 15 ounces per gallon), but there should be some undissolved lime in the bath as a reserve. The same lime solution can be used several times, and it is better to start the liming with a used solution. In a used lime solution, there are breakdown products from previously dehaired hides; these increase the lime's ability to penetrate and loosen the hypodermis, or, mucous layer, which makes the dehairing go faster and the hides swell less. When the hide's fibers swell, a mechanical loosening takes place in the hide; when the fibers shrink again, there remains an empty space which leaves room for the tanning agents. A certain amount of swelling is therefore desirable. On the other hand, if the swelling is too great, it can result in the grain's being rumpled and the hair-roots' remaining in the follicles after dehairing.

If an old lime bath is not available, the new bath can be made a little milder by adding about 2% of common table salt (20 grams per liter of lime bath, or about 19 ounces per gallon). The salt acts to inhibit the swelling.

It is important to stir the lime bath daily; if the hide sits in a too-weak lime bath it can rot from within. When the undissolved lime in the bath is used up, more must be added so that the solution is always supersaturated. Always remove the hide when new lime is added and stir the bath before putting the hide back in.

Maintain a constant temperature for both the lime bath and the water rinses that follow. A temperature above 30°C (about 85°F) or below 10°C (about 50°F) can cause too much swelling, which can make the grain brittle.

A method that has been used in chamois production and elsewhere is to smear the hide with a paste of lime and water on the flesh side, fold it with the flesh side in and pack it in a bowl, then pour a weak lime solution over it. This method is also relatively mild, since the lime penetrates the hide slowly. When the hair comes out easily, the hide is taken out of the bath and dehaired. Too much time in the lime bath can cause the boundary layer between the grain and the underlying layers of the hide to dissolve, so that the grain can be rubbed off. This has been exploited in the production of chamois leather, where the grain is removed to get a soft velvety surface on both sides.

The limed, dehaired hide resembles a pork rind, and in its swollen state it is a good idea to scrub the flesh side to clean it of membranes. The hide should not be left exposed to air for long since calcium carbonate can precipitate out on the surface and form lime spots which can be seen on vegetable-tanned leather as irregular dull spots.

After dehairing, rinse the hide in a weak lime solution. So as not to shock the hide, reduce the amount of lime in the rinse water gradually for about an hour. Then rinse for a couple of hours in clean water, preferably running water.

If you want extra soft leather, you can put it in a fresh lime bath for a couple of days after the scrubbing step.

De-liming is done for the most part with water. But water will not dissolve out all the lime. After several hours of rinsing in water, about 1/3 of the lime will remain in a fairly stable union with the hide, and must be dissolved out chemically. This is especially important for vegetable tanning and alum-tawing. The vegetable tanning will not be completed if the hide contains lime. In alum-tawing, calcium can bond to the sulfate in the alum (potassium aluminum sulfate) to form calcium sulfate, and precipitate out as gypsum.

Nowadays, de-liming is an independent process which is done with weak acids such as lactose, acetic acid, or ammonium salts of these acids. In traditional tanning, de-liming was included as a part of several other processes.

Puering

Puering, from the word puer or purin, meaning urine, is seen as one of the hardest jobs in a tannery; it requires long experience and acute observation. In 1907 Dr. Otto Röhm took out a patent for using a pancreatic extract to produce a puering agent; before that, chicken, dog, and pigeon dung were primarily used. These dung puers can act as de-limers to a certain extent, but the process is primarily enzymatic. In the dung there are enzymes whose function is to break down food so that the body can utilize the nutrients. In puering, the tanner uses the enzymes which, by breaking down the elastin fibers and other unwanted proteins, bring about a loosening and flexibility and give the finished leather a smoother and more elastic grain. Puering, which is the final cleaning process for the hide before the actual tanning, is used primarily in conjunction with vegetable tanning and glacé tanning.

It is said that the best puer is made from white dog dung from Constantinople, but I usually use hen manure which is a little easier to work with and much easier to get hold of.

Mix in 1 part hen manure with about 10 parts water; let it ferment for 2-3 days. Pour out the liquid into a new container and try to avoid pouring in any of the solid particles. Lay the skin in the liquid. If there is not enough space in the bath and the puer is very strong, the skin can become discolored, so be somewhat careful if you are making white skins.

It is hard to say precisely how much time is needed, but 1-3 days is a good rule of thumb. The hide should return to its natural thickness and easily show impressions from your fingers {fig. 57}.

Fig. 57: Squeeze a fold of the hide between your fingers. If the puering is finished, the impression of your fingers should remain in the hide when you let go.

Bran Bate

The bran bate is used with oil tanning, but primarily with alum and glacé tanning and then after dung puering. When bran ferments in water it forms acids such as lactose and acetic acid. These acids act as delimers. Tanners talk about "sour" and "sweet" bran puers.

In a sweet bran bate the bran is stirred into lukewarm water and the skin is laid directly into it; the skin ferments together with the bran, which causes carbonic acid fermentation within the hide, loosening it and making it more receptive of the tanning agents. In a sour bran bate, one waits until the fermentation has begun and the acids are formed before adding the skin.

In older literature, there are warnings that these sour bran puers can go over into butyric acid fermentation, which makes the skin brittle. The risk is viewed as greatest in stormy weather, and to soften the influences one can add a little salt, which limits acid swelling in the skin; the process will take a little longer then.

If the bran contains meal, it increases the risk of the wrong type of fermentation. One way to guard against this is to rinse the bran first in water to remove any meal it may contain.

Bran bate, calculated for one sheepskin:

500 grams (about 18 ounces) bran
5 liters (about 1 1/3 gallons) water
50 grams (about 2 ounces) salt

Let the skin sit in the bate 1-3 days; it is finished when the hide floats up to the surface. I use primarily the sweet bran bate.

Pickling
Pickling is used in conjunction with chromium tanning and consists of treatment with an acid in a strong salt solution. The most commonly used acids are sulfuric acid and formic acid. Pickling preserves the hide and makes it receptive to chromium salts.

The process that begins with bark tanning, when the hides are first put in an old soured bark-liquor is, to a certain extent, comparable to pickling. Organic acids, e.g. lactic and acetic acid, that are formed by fermentation in the bark-liquor, work to de-lime, swell and preserve the skins.

Sole leather, which must be tight and compact, is dehaired in lime and rinsed for a time in water before it is put in an old bark-liquor whose acids act as a de-limer.

A raw-tanned and incompletely-tanned skin which has first been put in an old bark-liquor is, through the action of these acids, preserved in its middle.

62

TANNING

The Swedish word *garva*, to tan, comes originally from the German word *gerben*, meaning "to make complete".

What is generally meant by tanned leather, is a hide prepared such that it resists rotting to the greatest possible extent when wet, and keeps the strength, flexibility and suppleness of raw skin when dry.

A tanned hide should bear getting wet and be able to regain its leathery feel when it dries. A raw hide is troublesome to handle. It is hard and stiff when dry, and when wet it is easily attacked by microorganisms, bacteria and fungi; it rots and smells bad.

To become what we recognize as leather and fur, the skins must go through a series of processes that change the structure of its fibers.

It is hard to tell what methods tanners used in ancient times. There is a serious shortage of written sources, because of the self-evident nature of the tanning process, and also because it was women's work, and thus there was no need to write it down.

We can, however, get some idea of how tanning took place in Mesopotamia between 1000 and 600 B.C. from the following two recipes:

"This skin, you will take it, then you will drench it in pure pulverized Nisaba flour, in water, beer and first quality wine. With the best fat of a pure ox, the alum of the land of the Hittites and oak-galls you will press it and you will cover the bronze kettle-drum with it.

"You will steep the skin of a young goat with the milk of a yellow goat and with flour. You will anoint it with pure oil, ordinary oil and fat of a pure cow. You will soak the alum in grape juice and then cover the surface of the skin with gall nuts collected by the tree-growers of the land of the Hittites." [Reed, 1972: 88f].

The recipes contain all the steps of the tanning process. The flour is ground grain; solutions of grain, fruits and berries yield a weakly basic liquid that contains enzymes and acts as a dehairer. If the bath is not heated too much the enzymes continue to loosen up the skin, corresponding to puering and bating. Beer and wine ferment the bath, which becomes acidic, swells the hide and lets the yeast-fungi's enzyme systems act on the hide and make it receptive to tanning. The fat works both to tan and lubricate; the alum functions as a bate and makes it easier for the tanning and dyeing agents to penetrate the hide. The galls contain vegetable tanning agents, and the end result is a combination-tanned skin.

The reason these complex methods were abandoned might have to do with an increased demand for a uniformly good result, and that it was easier to control the processes if they were carried out in separate baths. The recipes appearing in this book build on a multiple-bath system.

63

"Chemical" tanning agents

In the 19th century there arose a great interest and need for chemical research. This affected the tanning industry as well, and in the middle of the century the tanning properties of chromium salts were discovered. Chromium-tanned leather is supple and has a high resistance to hot, even boiling, water, with a greater water-absorbency than vegetable-tanned leather. Chromium-tanned leather has a gray-green to blue-gray color, but can be overdyed easily.

In the 20th century there have appeared a series of chemical tanning agents, such as formaldehyde, quinone and synthetic tanning agents. The synthetically constructed tanning agents, called syntans, cannot completely replace vegetable tanning agents, but they can be used to speed up the process. In the synthetic tanning agents one can obtain small molecules that penetrate the hide easily and, if you will, "open the way" for the vegetable tanning agents.

Oil tanning

"Grease- and smoke-tanning is probably the only tanning method used by prehistoric Man in the interglacial period in Europe." [Gansser, 1950: 2943].

Fats have a softening influence on leather just as they do on our own skin. If grease is worked into leather, it will become softer because the fibers will be surrounded by a protective envelope and are thus held apart from each other. The grease fills the space between the fibers and yields a leather that is more watertight, but that does not insulate as well against cold. Most fats do not bond to the leather but can easily be washed out. Certain fats, those that are unsaturated and are able to oxidize, can under certain favorable conditions of heat, acidity and mechanical processing, enter into a chemical bond with the hide. The result is a yellowish, porous and soft leather. This leather has a great water-absorbing capacity, but can then be dried and returned to its earlier state.

There is a lot of information concerning the greases that were used, for example brain grease, fish eggs, sea-birds' eggs, industrial olive oil (a by-product of olive oil production), rapeseed oil, and rancid butter.

Chamois leather

The term *sämskläder*, chamois leather, comes from the German word *Sämischleder*, which in turn is derived from the Dutch word *Seem*, meaning "soft". The French and English word is chamois leather; "chamois" is the French word for the chamois goat. Deer, roe, goat, sheep, and elk skins can be chamois-tanned. By chamois-leather is meant an oil-tanned skin with the grain split off. Only small, thin skins have been chamois- tanned with a grain.

Chamois tanning came to Sweden from Europe. In the 17th century chamois-makers formed their own guild,, and in the 18th century the profession was one of the most common in the cities. Chamois-tanned skins are soft, durable and easy to wash. The skins were used in clothing for trousers, vests and gloves, among other things.

As recently as 1960 there was a chamois-tannery in Ensta, on the Fyris River in Uppland. The following description of how chamois-leather was made at this tannery was related to me by Erik Flink, who worked there as a tanner until it closed.

The tanners began by softening the hides in water for several days. The softened hides were taken up and smeared on the flesh side with a lime suspension, about the same consistency as paint. The hides were folded up and laid in a vat, then water was poured over them. There they lay for about a month before they were taken out and dehaired. The hair was washed and sold as stuffing to upholsterers; reindeer-hair was used for mattresses. The hides were then laid in a fresh, weak lime solution for a few weeks, after which the flesh side was scraped clean. Back in the lime bath again for a couple of weeks, until the boundary layer was dissolved between the grain and the underlying dermis, so that the grain could be removed. After rinsing in water, the remaining lime-water was wrung out of the hide with a special wringer. After wringing out, the hides were placed in the stamper {fig. 58}.

Fig. 58. Hammarvalk stamping machine, sketched after A. Berglund, 1900:563.

Train-oil was poured into the chamber and the hides were worked for several hours, until all the oil was absorbed by the hides, which were then hung up and allowed to dry a bit. The oil was gotten by cutting seal fat into chunks or strips that were boiled in a large pot to a fine, clear oil. The residue was filtered out.

The hides were worked in the stamper 4-5 times and were dried between times. Toward the end of the tanning process, which could take a couple of weeks, a strong heat build up took place, which meant that the hides had to be watched carefully so that they would not burn. When the tanning was finished, the surplus grease was washed out with soda. The hides were washed several times; between each washing, they were wrung out on the wringer. The wrung-out wash-water, called fat-lye, is saved. Before the hides were dried and softened they had to be re-greased, which was done by dipping the washed hides in a mix made from the fat-lye from the second wringing and water. The hides were wrung once more by hand and hung up to dry.

By adding a little sulfuric acid to the remaining fat-lye, the fat was made to crystallize out and collect on the surface. This fat, called degras, was sold to tanners and used as a leather grease.

Some tanners let the hides go through a bran bate before the greasing, to dissolve out the remaining lime and make the skin more porous. The lime remaining in the hide can bond with the fatty acids supplied during tanning and form insoluble lime soaps, which make for a tighter leather.

By letting the hide go through a bran bate, one gets a very soft skin after tanning, so soft that it is even thought to be too soft for some products.

Another example of grease-tanned leather is the so-called crown leather. In 1852, a German by the name of Klemm arrived at a method of producing a leather that was lighter, but stronger and tighter than bark-tanned leather.

The dehaired hides are dried somewhat and then smeared with a mixture consisting of:

   20 parts barley meal
   23 parts ox or cow brains
    4 parts kitchen salt
    6 1/2 parts unsalted butter
   12 1/2 parts milk
   24 parts horse lard or neats foot oil

Blend the butter and brains first, then add the meal, and then the grease, and lastly the milk. The salt can be added at any time and functions only as a preservative for the mixture. Heat the mixture and work it into the hide in several applications. [Recipe from Schmidt 1871: 22]

An example of leather tanned with vegetable oil is the so-called Japan leather tanned with rapeseed oil. Hides from cattle, for example, are laid in the river until the hair comes out; the hair is saved and used for blankets. The women spread salt on the hides and tread it in with river water; the hides are then left to lie in the sun for several days, until most of the moisture has disappeared. The women smear the hides with rapeseed oil which is trodden in, and then the hides are left in the sun; the process is repeated several times, until the skins take on a reddish-brown color. The hides are washed again and the surplus oil is rinsed out by working the hides with bundles of wheat-straw. The hides are rinsed in the river again, dried slowly, and softened; then they are left to rest for 2-4 weeks before they are rinsed again in the river, dried and softened. The result is a bright and strong skin that is used for bags, sandals and gloves. This recipe comes from the book *Ledertechnik in Zeit und Raum*.

66

Chemistry

A fat consists of a glycerol unit and 3 fatty acids. These fatty acids are arranged like a pitchfork with three tines {Figs. 59a & b}.

Fig. 59a. Pitchfork.

The fatty acids can be either saturated or unsaturated, that is they can either lack or have double bonds in the carbon chain {Fig. 60}.

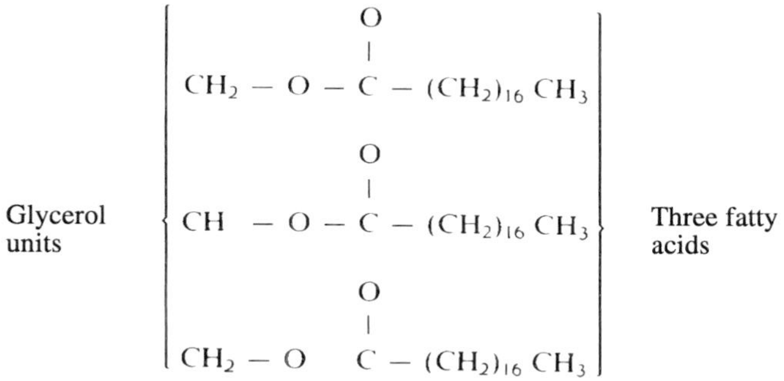

$$
\text{Glycerol units} \left\{ \begin{array}{l} \overset{\displaystyle O}{\underset{|}{CH_2 - O - C}} - (CH_2)_{16}\,CH_3 \\[2mm] \overset{\displaystyle O}{\underset{|}{CH \ \ - O - C}} - (CH_2)_{16}\,CH_3 \\[2mm] \overset{\displaystyle O}{\underset{|}{CH_2 - O \ \ \ \ C}} - (CH_2)_{16}\,CH_3 \end{array} \right\} \text{Three fatty acids}
$$

Fig. 59b. Example of a fat, glyceryltristearate, with glycerol units on the left and three fatty acid units on the right.

$$- CH2 - CH = CH - CH2 - CH2 -$$

Fig. 60. Example of double bonds in a fatty acid's carbon chain.

Through the influence of oxygen, these double bonds can be split up and can bond to oxygen atoms instead {fig. 61}.

The products formed in this oxidation process, aldehydes, react further with the amino groups on the collagen chains and cross-link the parts of the fibers to each other; this tans the hide{fig. 62a, p. 36}. This process is accelerated by heat (the molecules gain more kinetic energy) and by mechanical working.

$$- CH2 - CH = CH - CH2 - + O2$$

$$\begin{array}{cc} O & O \\ \parallel & \parallel \\ - CH2 - CH & + CH - CH2 - CH2 - \end{array}$$

Fig. 61. Oxidation of double bond in a fatty acid to form aldehydes (simplified process).

The process of rancidity is a form of self-oxidation, which is why a rancid fat reacts more easily with the hide than a fresh one.

The collagen chains' reactive amino groups appear in a basic or neutral hide as NH_2. On the other hand, if the hide is acidic, then the amino groups bond to hydrogen ions to form NH_3+, a bond that has more trouble reacting with fatty acids. One way to facilitate and accelerate the course of the tanning process is thus to supply the hide with a base, such as soap, whose OH- group reacts with any surplus hydrogen ions, H+, to form water, so that the amino groups go back to NH_2 {fig. 62b, p. 45}. One conclusion of this is that hides that have been dehaired with lime, which is basic, react more easily with the fatty acids, especially if the hide has not been fully delimed.

Washing oil-tanned hides in soap or soda has two effects:

1. The basic OH- groups react with any surplus hydrogen ions, H+, in the amino groups; the fatty acids react more easily and the tanning will be more complete.

2. Excess fat is washed away so that the finished hide does not feel greasy.

Iodine count

If one supplies iodine to an unsaturated fat, the unsaturated parts of the fat molecule will take up the iodine and become saturated. By measuring how much iodine a fat is able to bond, one can get an idea of the fat's level of unsaturation. This is called the "iodine count".

The iodine count for certain oils is very high (linseed oil, 172-196) while for solid fats it is low (beef tallow, 32-47). When hot, oils with a very high iodine count, such as linseed oil, react easily with oxygen in the air, and can ignite spontaneously under certain circumstances.

Linseed oil is used in the production of lacquer for patent leather.

When saturated fats, e.g. tallow and lard, are used, the fat lies between the fibers and has more of a lubricating than a tanning effect on the hide, which is why fats with a low iodine count are more properly used as a fat liquor than a tanning agent.

The more double bonds, the higher the iodine count, the lower the melting temperature a fat has; that is, the fat stays soft even at a low temperature. These fats are called oils. In order to survive in cold water, many aquatic animals have unsaturated fats. Useful oils for tanning are, for example:

cod liver oil	iodine count 140-181
seal train oil	iodine count 122-162
rapeseed oil	iodine count 80-85
olive oil	iodine count 98.6

These iodine counts are typical, though different researchers have published slightly different ranges, based on the samples available to them.

The finished leather's color varies from almost white to yellow. A fat that oxidizes and bonds to the hide easily yields a yellower leather.

Phospholipids are a family of fats that have a polar end with an electric charge{Fig. 63}. This gives them the ability to dissolve in water, which also has a distributed charge, according to the principle of "like dissolves like". In solution, the phospholipids form small drops, called micells. These micells resemble a ball with its charged ends outwards and its un-charged fatty acids in the middle. The phospholipids can be both saturated and unsaturated. Brain and egg yolk are examples of materials that contain phosoholipids; brain is an excellent tanning agent, while egg yolk (iodine count 64-82) is used primarily as a lubricant. Phosoholipids are easy to work into the hide and can help draw in other, more solid fats.

The Indians of North America mix lard with brain substance. By first making a solution of water and brain substance, and then stirring and breaking up the micells, the melted lard's uncharged fatty acids get encapsulated in the middle of the "ball" and follow along into the hide {Fig. 64}.

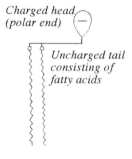

Charged head (polar end)

Uncharged tail consisting of fatty acids

Fig. 63. Example of a phospholipid.

If one mixes soap in as well, then the formation of micells becomes even more stable. The same principle is used in doing the dishes; that is, the fat on the plate is encapsulated in small balls of detergent which dissolve in water and can be rinsed away.

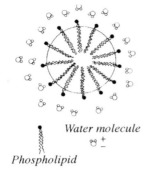

Fig. 64. A phospholipid dissolved in water, forming micells.

Water molecule

$\underset{-}{\overset{+}{}}$

Phospholipid

Native American Brain tanning of moose and deer hide

The following recipe is based on the knowledge I received from Helen Tobie and Clara Yellowknife as well as my own experience.

The method calls for little equipment and a relatively short time. Do not use too large a piece the first time you set out to tan a moose hide. Half of a yearling skin is about right. Divide the skin along the line of the backbone. The hide is thickest at the neck and along the back line. A full-grown moose has much thicker skin than a calf.

Begin by soaking the hide in water. If the hide has been salted and you have no running water, then change the water in the pot a couple of times the first day and once a day after that. When the hair can be pulled loose, stretch the hide on a frame. The longer the hide sits in the water, the more easily the hair will come out; but since a rotting process is going on, the finished leather will be weaker the longer the process continues.

Scrape off the hair with an iron scraper [Fig. 46, p. 50].
If there is a thick membrane layer on the flesh side, chop it away with the bone scraper [Fig. 45a, p. 96], while the hide is still wet. When the hide has dried halfway, scrape the flesh side one more time with the iron scraper.

The next step is to scrape off the grain. This is done with the iron scraper when the hide is nearly dry. It is important that the hide have the right degree of moisture. If the hide is too wet it is almost impossible to remove the grain, and if it is too dry it is easy to make holes. It is a good idea to keep a plant sprayer full of water at hand.

Fat liquoring

The most effective fat liquor is thought to be brain. Tradition holds that "the animals brain should be enough to tan its skin". But it doesn't really matter what kind of brain is used, and the brain can also be

70

supplemented with train oil. Half of a cow or moose brain and 3 dl (about 1 1/4 cup) train oil is usually sufficient for a yearling calf.

It is better to have too much grease than too little. First rinse the brain in cold water to remove any blood.

Then boil the brain in 1/2 liter (about 1 pint) water until it becomes white, approx. 5 minutes. Mash the brain in the water and mix in the oil and 1 deciliter (about 1/2 cup) soap. If you cannot get hold of brain, train oil alone can also be used. Work half of the lukewarm solution into the grain side of the almost-dry hide.

The temperature of the mix should be around 30°C (about 85°F). Work the grease in with your hands or a wooden stick. Keep the hide warm, but not above 40°C (about 105°F), preferably over a fire or in the sunshine, and let the grease soak in for several hours {fig. 65}.

Work the hide at regular intervals. Soak the hide in lukewarm soapy water, about 1 deciliter (about 1/2 cup) soap per 10 liters (about 2 3/4 gallons) water. Crush the stiff hide down into the tub and it will soften. A plastic tub works well. When the hide is fully softened, lay it on the beam and scrape it with an old file {fig. 66}. This is how to remove dark tinges in the hide that come from shaved-off hair roots. Remove any remains of the fiber network by scraping the flesh side as well.

Then wash the hide in more soapy water. Work the skin in the bath by, for example, treading around barefoot in the tub.

Fig. 65. The hide is heated over a fire.

71

Fig. 66. *Scraping an old moose hide with an old file.*

Let the hide sit in the soapy water until it is completely soft and white. You should be able to press air through the hide when it is ready {fig. 67}.

If the hide is not porous, then it is not tanned through and must be greased again. The hide can stay in the soapy water for a couple of days without trouble.

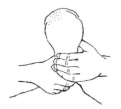

Fig. 67. *Make a pocket in the hide and try to press air through it.*

Softening

Fasten the hide together into a cylinder by threading a rope through the available holes. Wring out the hide using two poles, first crosswise and then lengthwise {fig. 68]}. If it is a large hide, stretch it out again

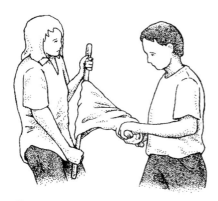

on the frame and work it for 30 minutes on each side by hitting it with a blunt instrument.

Tighten the rope as the hide stretches. Continue working the hide until it is nearly dry. Before the hide is taken down, clean it with sandpaper. Then cut the hide down from the frame. Cut right along the holes. Work the hide with an osier {fig. 86b, p. 97} until it is dry and soft. If it feels stiff and hard, it has dried too much on the frame; moisten it with water.

Fig. 68. Twisting out.

Smaller hides need not be stretched on a frame; rather, you can pull them and stretch them by hand {fig. 69}. If you do this you may want first to cut off the hard, often untanned, edge all the way around.

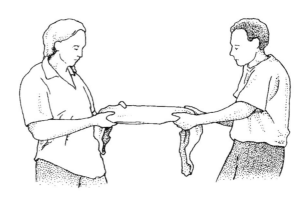

Fig. 69. Stretching a tanned hide.

73

Brain tanning thin skins
This method can also be used on thin skins if one wants to keep the grain. I have tried the method described here on reindeer, lamb, goat, and roe deer skins.

Dehairing and scraping
Dehair the skin with one of the methods described above [pp. 55-60]. Skins that have been dehaired with lime, and that you want to be extra soft, should also go through a bran bate [pp. 60, 61]. Scrape the flesh side thoroughly.

Greasing
For a reindeer skin:
Boil a reindeer brain about 5 minutes in 1/2 liter (about 1 pint) water, mix in 1/2 deciliter (about 1/4 cup) soap and 1 deciliter (about 1/2 cup) train oil. You can supplement the brain with extra train oil. Work the grease solution into the moist skin by folding the skin with the flesh side out, putting it in a pan and working it with your hands or with a wooden pestle{fig. 70}.

Keep the dish warm and work the skin regularly for a couple of hours. The skin can stay in the dish for a couple of days without trouble. Lift the skin up to expose it to air once or twice a day, and work it now and then.

When the tanning is finished, hang the skin up to dry. Work it while it is drying and then let it hang someplace warm for at least a couple of days, preferably a week or so.

Soaking
Lay the skin in soapy water, about 1 deciliter (about 1/2 cup) soap per 10 liters (about 2 3/4 gallons) water. Work the skin with your hands in the soap bath. The skin should sit in the bath until it is soft, white, and lets air through [Fig. 67, p. 72]. Overnight is usually enough time for the skin to sit. Change the water at least once.

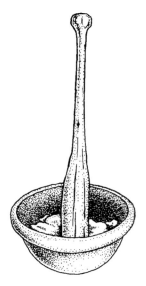

Softening
Remove and wring out the skin. Skin with a grain cannot be wrung out as hard as

Fig. 70. The skin is put in a dish and worked with a wooden pestle.

skin without a grain. Hang the skin up and let it dry halfway; soften it by pulling it through a drawing-osier {Fig. 86b, p. 97} or over a stake {Fig. 89, p. 98}. The skin should be soft and have a light yellow color. If the skin feels rough when it dries, moisten it a little and re-grease it with, for example, egg yolk.

Oil tanning furs

I have used this method with sheep and kid skin as well as on mountain suckling calf.

Scraping

Scrape the flesh side. If the fur is very dirty, first scrape off the worst of the flesh side and then wash the fur. Let the fur dry almost completely before you finish scraping the flesh side.

Fat liquoring

Work into the moist flesh side either boiled brain (boiled in water about 5 minutes), train oil or olive oil and a little soap. For a sheepskin, a teaspoon of soap and one mashed sheep brain or a couple of deciliters (about 1 cup) of oil should be enough. If the oil is also mixed with egg yolk it will penetrate better.

Work the grease in with your hands or with wooden sticks; it should be at a temperature of around 35°C (95°F). In old times, melted lard was used, or sheep tallow that was melted and heated by the fire; this was called *råberedning*, or raw-preparation. These fats do not bond chemically to the hide to the same extent as the unsaturated ones; rather, they lie between the fibers and lubricate them. Hang the skin in a warm place, maximum 40°C (about 105°F); work it at regular intervals. If the skin absorbs all the grease, then knead in some more. Let the skin hang with the grease on it for at least a couple of days; work it at regular intervals.

Soaking

Now wash the skin with soap. If the fur is dirty, it may need to be washed several times. The skin should sit in the soapy water until the flesh side is white and soft, which can take up to 4-5 hours. Rinse the soap out of the fur and wring out the skin.

Softening

When the fur has dried halfway, soften the skin by pulling it through a drawing osier, or by stretching it in the scraping rack.

Smoke Tanning

Smoke tanning has often appeared as a complement to oil tanning or vegetable tanning. The smoke impregnates the hide so that it becomes more watertight. A fat liquored and smoked hide which gets wet will not stiffen as it dries; rather, it will remain soft without mechanical working. It is usually dehaired hides that are smoked, but I have seen women who have smoked beaver-skins with fur. Smoking has been done in different ways by different peoples. The Chukchi had special smoke-sheds; in China they built brick ovens {fig. 71a}.

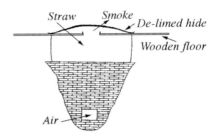

Fig. 71a. Smoke tanning oven from China (Tsai, 1929: 22).

The Indians of North America sew the hide up into a sack and pass the smoke through it, or else place the hide around a tripod. In Japan patterns have been made by placing stencils {fig. 73} or by stretching a rope across the hide and smoking it in several stages; the rope was moved in between smokings and various fuels were used to give the hide different colors.

With the help of different sorts of fuel, a smoldering fire with lots of smoke is produced. Fuels used include fir, poplar, cedar, oak-bark, straw, etc. For lots of smoke, the fuel should be decayed and somewhat damp.

Fig. 72. Japanese family crest. Template constructed of handmade Japanese paper smoked and tanned. The skin was smoked with straw.

Chemistry

In the smoke from burning wood there are a quantity of different materials, including aldehydes and quinones of various types and in different quantities, depending on what kind of wood is burned.

These different units display a certain similarity and have, among other things, a common group, $C=O$, carbonyl.

This group reacts with collagen's amino group (NH_2) to form a very stable bond.

If one compares the shrinkage temperatures of a smoke-tanned skin and one tanned with formalin, a solution of formaldehyde, one gets approximately the same result. This can possibly imply that the formaldehydes present in the smoke are what have the strongest tanning influence.

In the last decade it was discovered that formaldehyde fumes are dangerous and unhealthy. Formalin tanning is used to make other tanning methods more wear resistant, such as glacé tanning and chamois tanning.

Quinones have also been used for tanning. Quinone tanned skins stand up to high temperatures, even boiling, without shrinkage. They have a strong and irritating smell and the fumes are unhealthy, which may be the reason that quinone tanning has never achieved any great practical significance.

Smoking

When the hide is fully dry and soft it can be smoked. Smoking should be done on a still, clear, not too cold day. Below -10°C (about 15°F), condensation forms and the hide becomes damp. I usually smoke my skins with decayed spruce wood.

Sew up the hide into a pouch with one short side open. Sew a piece of fabric on the bottom and hang up the hide. Let a fire burn in a bucket until you have a bed of coals to lay the decayed wood on. Place the bucket under the hanging piece of cloth so that the smoke is guided up into the elkskin pouch.

When smoking small skins, it is easier to make a tripod. Use smooth, clean poles. The hides are attached inside the poles and the whole thing is covered with a cotton cloth which reaches the ground. Light the fire on the ground or in a bucket.

Have a pail of water and a bunch of fir twigs ready to hand, and never leave the hides during the smoking. It just takes a moment for the whole thing to burn up.

The smoking can take from 1/2 to 5 hours depending on how strong a color one wants and whether one wants to smoke only one side or both.

The Cree Indians, for example, smoke both sides, but wear the skins with the flesh side out. Put the fully smoked hide in a paper bag for a day so that the color will set {figs. 73 & 74, p. 78}.

Figs. 73 & 74. Smoke tanning.

Vegetable tanning Chemistry

A bark decoction for tanning contains a great quantity of substances dissolved in water, both tannins and non-tanning materials. The non-tanning materials are often made of different kinds of sugars as well as organic acid salts. The tanning substances are different tannins; it is these that give the solution a harsh taste, the more tannins the harsher the taste. The tannins are made up of large ring-shaped molecules with a number of reactive OH-groups; these groups are active in tanning.

Chemically speaking, the tannins can be classified as condensed or hydrolysable. The division depends on the difference in their basic structure, which makes them react differently when one tries to break them up. The condensed tannins are more astringent and tan more quickly than the hydrolysable. Condensed tannins make greenish-black spots on contact with iron, while hydrolysable tannins make bluish-black spots [Reed 1972:73f].

Mimosa, birch, sallow, alder and fir bark are examples of substances containing condensed tannins, while sumac and oak-wood, for example, contain hydrolysable tannins. Both types are found in oak bark.

78

The large tannin molecules penetrate into the collagen and bind together adjacent collagen chains into a network that is retained when the water disappears. The binding together takes place through the formation of hydrogen bridges between the tannins' OH-groups and oxygen- and hydrogen-atoms in the collagen chain, mainly in the primary chain, but also in side groups.

Vegetable tanning can be seen as a filling of the spaces between the collagen chains, and in a vegetable tanned hide the amount of tannin can reach 50% of the weight of the leather.

It is hard to determine how the leather found in archaeological excavations was tanned. Leather and skin that lies in the earth or in bogs is transformed by the often weakly acidic surroundings and by the vegetal substances that are present. That means, for example, that a skin which was originally alum tawed can, after a long time in a bog, have its alum salts leached out to be replaced by vegetable tannins.

We know that vegetable tanning has ancient roots, from traces found in Gebelein, Egypt, of a tannery that is thought to be over 5000 years old. There were tools and pieces of tanned and half-finished skin together with pods of *Acacia nilotica* (a sort of mimosa) and pieces of oak-bark [Gansser 1950: 2943].

There are tannins in wood, bark, fruit, roots, and certain diseased outgrowths. Plants containing tanning agents can be found all over the world. The tannin is found in small bladders in the living cells. In wood, the tannin is precipitated in the bark layer where it forms a barrier against microorganisms such as fungi and bacteria.

The tannins' affect on microorganisms can be seen when one places a skin which has been dehaired by sweating into a tanning solution. The bacteria become tanned and die, the breaking-down process stops and the sour odor disappears.

It has also been observed that plants spread tannins in the earth to prevent the growth of competitors; however, the various aspects of the tannins' function are far from being understood.

In hospitals, tannins have been used to protect burn injuries. They transform the skins' proteins, the ends of the nerve cells become tanned, and the pain is soothed. Tannin has the properties of a weak acid; it has a harsh astringent taste, oxidizes easily in air and forms a blue or black precipitation when exposed to iron.

Warning! *Vegetable tanned leather that comes into contact with iron can get black spots; these may in certain circumstances be neutralized with oxalic acid, but are difficult to get rid of completely .*

Vegetable tanning amounts to getting the tannic acid to bond chemically with the hide. Vegetable tanned leather is durable, soft and water resistant.

The method thought to be the oldest is the so-called sprinkle-tanning. A hide is laid in a hole in the ground or in a vat, after which it is sprinkled with finely ground moistened bark, the next hide is spread on top of it, more bark is sprinkled over it, and so on until the hole is filled. Then water or an old bark-liquor is poured over it and the whole is covered with a lid. The tannin is slowly extracted from the bark and bonds with the hides. This method takes up to two years for coarser hides; the bark is changed 3-4 times. At first old and fresh bark are mixed; towards the end only fresh bark is used.

Holes discovered in Heinheim, Bavaria and dated to 6200-5000 B.C. may have been used for sprinkle-tanning [van de Velde, 1937: 58].

No great transformations in the techniques of leather preparation took place from ancient times up to the end of the 18th century. The demand for shoe leather grew then and attempts were made to increase production efficiency. In revolutionary France a trained tanner named Armand Seguin was considered the organizer of tanners and investigator of tanning. He showed that the hide after tanning increases in weight and thus that tanning material was absorbed into the hide.

Earlier, the common impression was that the tannin caused a drying-out and contraction of the hide. Seguin came to the conclusion that tanning was best done with concentrated solutions and not with tanning substances in solid form, which had earlier been the norm. Seguin's suggestion was received with great acclaim and led to the use of extracts taken from plants with a high concentration of tannins such as Mimosa, Quebracho and Sumac.

Tanning time was shortened and the new method came to be called *snällgarvning*, "quick-tanning" (from the German *schnell* = quick).

Bark tanning

Vegetable tanning was once called *logarvning* (German *Lohe* = bark) since it is often from bark that the tannins are taken. The most usual homemade tanning substances come from oak, fir, sallow, birch, rowan and alder. Bearberry (leaves), heather, bloodroot, sweet gale, and wood-hops have also been used to a lesser extent.

The tannin is generally located in the inner bark. It is easiest to peel off in the springtime, and that is also the time of year when the bark contains the most tannic acid. As a rule it makes no difference if the outer bark remains, but with birch it must be taken off. Coarse fir bark should also be cleaned. the bark is dried and cut into small pieces before use. There are a number of different machines and tools to break up the bark; there have been slicing machines, crushing machines and mills {fig. 75}. The more finely the bark is divided, the more tannin can be gotten from it.

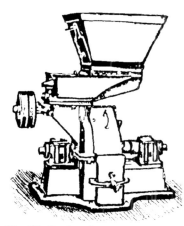

Fig. 75. Bark mill.

Oak bark is one of our most important tanning materials. The average tannin content is 10%. The wood also contains considerable quantities of tannic acid, around 6%. The sugar content is about 25%. The bark of the oak tree contains the most tannin when the tree has reached an age between 15 and 30 years. Oak-bark-tanned leather has long been considered mellow and tight, with a pretty yellow-brown color and dark cross-section.

Fir bark is the one bark available throughout Sweden. According to 19th-century sources, the tree should have reached the age of 30 years before the bark is peeled off. The tannin content reaches around 11%. Fir bark is, after birch bark, our most sugary tanning material, containing about 35% sugar. Through the fermentation of the sugar, organic acids are formed that can be advantageous in the early stages of tanning. Fir bark yields a yellow-brown leather.

Sallow and willow bark are counted as the best barks for tanning purposes. They yield a soft, supple and bright leather. Tannin content lies around 10% and sugar content is about 25%.

Birch bark yields a somewhat fragile leather, probably because it dissolves out the hide's natural greases. The tannin content is about 12% and the sugar content about 40%. The bark is used mostly in combination with other barks and is sought for its high sugar content. The bark gives a light red-brown color to the leather.

Rowan bark has not been used to any great extent, but yields a soft and bright leather.

Alder bark yields a hard and fragile leather and has primarily been used to color leather that is already tanned. It gives a gray-brown to red-brown color; the strongest color comes from the bark of the roots.

Tanners have a golden rule that is important to follow, especially when tanning thick hides. This rule states that one should always start the tanning with a weak tanning bath and then gradually increase the strength.

The tanning bath contains tannin particles of varying size. When a hide is laid down in a fresh, strong tanning bath, the larger particles settle on its surface and block up the hide's pores, which prevents the smaller particles from penetrating into the hide. The hide becomes thoroughly tanned on the outside, but the inner parts remain raw; this is

81

called "dead-tanning". To avoid this, the first tanning bath should preferably be a used one, the larger particles already used up. The strength of the bath is then increased successively, by which the tanning processes advance slowly.

The tannin particles' molecular weight, meaning their size, increase along with the concentration of the solution. If you have no used bark liquor, you can use a weak, fresh liquor.

The sugar found in the bark can, in an old bark liquor, begin to ferment; this forms organic acids such as lactic and acetic acid. These acids have a deliming, swelling and preserving effect. The deliming effect is exploited in the tanning of leather that has been delimed only in water and therefore contains lime bonded to the hide. The raw stripe, that is the untanned layer that is left in the middle of the hide in the production of raw-tanned leather, is to a certain extent preserved through the influence of these acids. These acid baths have been used primarily with the production of tighter leathers, such as sole leather.

Chemistry

A bark decoction for tanning contains a great quantity of substances dissolved in water, both tannins and non-tanning materials.

The non-tanning materials are often made of different kinds of sugars as well as organic acid salts. The tanning substances are different tannins; it is these that give the solution a harsh taste, the more tannins the harsher the taste. The tannins are made up of large ring-shaped molecules with a number of reactive OH-groups; these groups are active in tanning {fig. 76}.

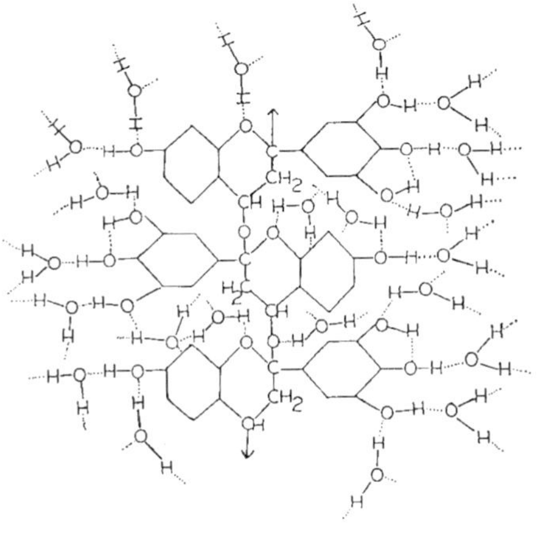

Fig. 76. Example of a hydrolysable tannin. The numerous OH groups bond to the collagen with weak hydrogen bonds. The dotted lines from the oxygen and hydrogen atoms show where the bonds can occur.

Dehairing and scraping

Dehair the skin with one of the methods given earlier. Skin that has been dehaired with lime will be softer if it is puered before tanning.

Flesh the skin. It does not need to be completely fleshed before it goes into the first tanning bath; rather, it can be taken out between baths and fleshed.

Tanning

I have used this method on reindeer, goat, sheep, pig, deer, and roe-deer skin. For thin hides you can use a fresh, relatively strong bath from the beginning, but the results are better if you follow the golden rule.

Boil up a bark liquor. Fill a kettle halfway with bark and pour water over it up to the edge of the kettle. Do not use an iron kettle, and preferably avoid tap water which can contain rust. Bring it to a boil and let it boil for at least an hour.

Taste the bark liquor to monitor its strength. The more bitter the taste, the stronger the bark liquor is. The taste is the same as old, bitter tea; tea and coffee also contain tannin, tea up to 20% and coffee about 5%. Take half of the liquor and mix with an equal amount of water for the first tanning bath. If a used bath is available, use it as the first tanning bath. You can put the bath in a plastic or rust-proof tub. Historically, wooden vats were used.

Put the drained skin in the tanning bath. Stir it for the first 10 minutes and then once every 10 minutes for about an hour. As soon as the skin starts to take on color, you must be sure that the color is taking over the whole skin. If the skin develops white patches, it is because some of the epidermis remains and is blocking the entry of the tannins. The epidermis must then be scraped off; you can take off small spots with your nail, larger pieces should be taken off with a dull scraper. Be careful of the grain. The epidermis of sheepskin is usually extra troublesome to get rid of.

Stir the tanning bath every half hour. Let it stand at room temperature. After a few hours the rest of the boiled bark liquor can be added. Remove the skin when it has lain in the tanning bath for 4-5 hours. Let it dry a little and scrape it again. At this scraping, you should make sure that all the remaining membrane is removed. The skin can also be frozen for some time between the baths.

Boil more bark liquor and continue to strengthen the tanning bath. The old baths can be used to boil new bark in and in this fashion become all the stronger. Bark liquor used as a first bath for skin that was dehaired with lime can contain dissolved lime and should not be boiled again and used in later steps of the tanning process.

To remove as much tannic acid as possible from the bark, take bark that has already been boiled and boil it again in clean water, which yields a weak bark bath that can be used in the initial tanning steps.

When the whole skin has taken an even, brown color, the bark can be left in with the skin in the bath and you can also leave it for longer times without stirring it.

If the hides stay in too weak a tanning bath, they begin to rot from the inside. Once they are tanned through, there is no trouble with letting them stay in the bath.

The length of the tanning time is determined by cutting off a piece of the hide. Tanned leather has an even brown color in cross-section; untanned is white, almost bluish. The difference in color is more visible if you moisten the edges of the section. The inner, lighter stripe is weakly tanned if at all. The fiber is matted, glistening, and doesn't absorb the saliva when moistened. On a thin skin, it can be difficult to see the difference in color, and if you can then fold the skin double two times and press the folded area between your fingers, when the skin is unfolded the places where the fold was should appear as light dry lines {fig. 77}.

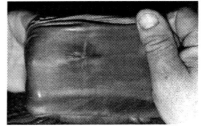

Fig. 77.

If you want to be quite sure how the final result will be, you can cut off a little piece of the hide, and dry and soften it. An untanned hide dries fast on the surface but remains moist inside. An untanned hide breaks easily in thinner areas.

A goatskin takes about 7-10 days to tan through. How much bark is used depends on the bark's tannin content, but about 4 - 5 kg (about 1 3/4 - 2 1/4 lbs.) of dried bark to one goatskin is a rule of thumb.

Cattle and elkhides, which are significantly larger and thicker, can take half a year to tan through. For these, it is simpler to layer powdered bark together with the hides in the tanning vat. Begin with a previously used bark liquor, stir the vat every day and fill it with new bark at least every ten days.

Thick hides used for sole-leather have been left with an untanned stripe in the middle, and thus been more water-tight and harder. Nowadays, leather with a raw stripe is used primarily for knife-sheaths.

Furs are prepared by rubbing in the bark liquor from the flesh side a number of times. The bark or a scrub-brush can be used to scrub with.

84

Between each tanning the skin is stretched out and allowed to dry; this is especially important in the tanning of reindeer skins,which begin to lose their hair if they are left damp for too long. By cutting into the skin, one can see how deeply the bark liquor has penetrated.

Finishing

The hides are taken out of the tanning bath, rinsed in fresh water for a couple of hours, dried a bit, greased and softened. In a craft tannery, the finishing of cowhides could take place as in the description below.

Oiling and washing

The tanned and rinsed hide was laid up on the tanning table, which could be made of wood with a zinc or copper cover. The hide was laid with the flesh side up and rubbed with a sleeker {fig. 78}, to press out as much water as possible and to get the hide to lay smooth on the table.

The hide was smeared with a mixture of equal parts of tallow and train oil, turned and rubbed with a slate-bladed washing-stone on the grain side. Then the exposed grain side was smeared with train oil and the hide was hung up to dry.

Fig. 78. Blunt edged sleeker.

Currying

When the hide was dry it was taken down again so that if necessary it could be shaved, that is, pared down to an even thickness. This was done on a flat, sloping surface with a currier's knife {fig. 79}. This knife has two edges and sharpening it is a difficult art. First a sharp edge is honed, whose outermost millimeter is bent at a 90° angle. The knife is moved diagonally forward. Currying could also be done before the tanning; this was called lime-currying.

85

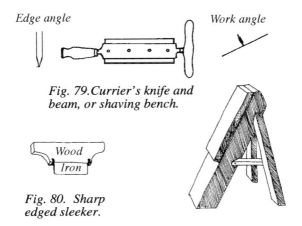

Edge angle   Work angle

Fig. 79.Currier's knife and
beam, or shaving bench.

Wood
Iron

Fig. 80. Sharp
edged sleeker.

Sleeking
The sleeking iron {Fig. 80} has a wooden handle and a steel blade, and is used to even out the hide and get a smooth and fine flesh side.

Softening
The hide is softened with a stake or a graining board {see under softening, pp. 48, 98 and 99}.

Grain patterning
Different types of grain-rollers {fig. 81} were used to make patterns in the grain.

Fig. 81. Grain roller.

Glazing
Glazing is done when the hide is otherwise finished; the grain side is rubbed with a weak soap solution and is then scrubbed with a washing stone whose blade consists of a plate of glass{fig. 82}.
Glazing produces a tight and shiny grain.

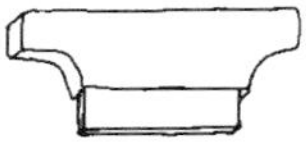

Fig. 82. Sleeker with
glass blade.

86

Alum tawing

In warm areas like the Middle East, Africa and Asia, alum appears freely in nature. Wind and rain cause rocks containing aluminum-rich slate to wear down slowly, with the result that alum is spread into the sea and the earth. Alum-tawing is the oldest inorganic tanning method.

Following the excavations of graves in Ur, Mesopotamia, it was learned that Queen Schub-ad and her ladies in waiting wore diadems made of small lapis lazuli stones held together with leather bands that were alum tawed, perhaps in combination with galls and fat. The graves date back to about 2700 B.C. [Frendrup, 89: 12; Larsson, 78: 65].

Alum tawing was brought to Europe by the Moors* in the 8th century [Gustavsson, 1943: 12]. In Sweden the method first became common in the 12th century, and up to the beginning of our century seal-leather, upper leather, gloves and furs were tawed with alum. Starting in the 20th century, alum tawing has for the most part been replaced with chromium tanning.

Tawing yields a product that is white, supple and stretchable, but unstable in water; the process can better be likened to preservation rather than tanning of the hide. The tawing medium, the so-called bate, is made of alum, 8-10%, table salt, 3-5% and water, 60-100%, all compared to the weight of a limed, dehaired skin. The bate penetrates the skin in a few hours' time. The skins are hung up to dry without rinsing, and aged for a few weeks or months for greater stability. Alum tawed leather withstands heat poorly, even worse than untanned leather.

The alum tawing can be made more durable by adding other substances such as egg, oil, flour and vegetable substances.

A Swedish specialty used for gloves and shoe uppers was *Svenskläder* ("Swedish leather"), which was tanned with a combination of alum tawing and vegetable tanning.

Alum stabilizes the grain and inhibits the formation of cracks. Glacé tanning is a kind of alum tawing in which egg yolk, oil and wheat flour are included as so-called nutritive substances. The oil and egg yolk lubricate the fibers and tans to a certain extent; the flour binds the fat and makes the skin plumper. Vegetable-dyeing works well with alum-tawed skins.

Chemistry

Alum appears as a mineral in many places. Alum, or potassium aluminum sulfate, is a double salt of potassium and aluminum {Fig. 83} and it is the aluminum ions and sulfate ions which react with the collagen; for this reason the leather industry uses aluminum sulfate instead of alum.

$$AlK(SO_4)_2 \cdot 12\,H_2O$$

Fig. 83: The double salt alum; potassium aluminum sulfate.

When aluminum sulfate is dissolved in water it bonds with OH-ions from the water, freeing hydrogen ions. In the solution, the basic aluminum sulfate appears as a molecule complex plus sulfuric acid. Because of its size and structure, the molecule complex bonds only to a limited extent with the hide, which through the bonding exerts a limited tanning influence. The bonds are weak and the finished leather has poor resistance to water, but on the other hand it is very supple and soft.

The tanning works best if the hide is acidic, pH 3-5; for this reason many recipes today include formic acid, which acts as a preservative and places the hide within a correct pH range. Sulfuric acid swells the hide; salt is therefore added as a swelling inhibitor.

Tanning in a bath of alum, salt and water

This method can be used for tanning or fur preparation. I have tanned reindeer, goat and sheepskin, and prepared goat, sheep, hare, rabbit, marten, mink, and beaver skins as furs by this method with good results. For hides that lose their hair easily, such as reindeer and elk hides, I recommend the paste method {p. 90}.

Scraping, dehairing and washing

Scrape the flesh side. Dehair the skins to be tanned using one of the given methods. Skins dehaired with lime can be puered if desired, and delimed with bran bate. Dried skins to be prepared as furs are soaked first in salted water, 1 dl (about 1/2 cup) salt per 10 liters (about 2 3/4 gallons) water. Wash the furs. Scrape the flesh side again, though they do not need to be thoroughly scraped at this stage.

Alum bating

This recipe is calculated for a short-haired or dehaired sheepskin.
Dissolve 300 grams (about 2 1/4 ounces) of aluminum sulphate and 150 grams (about 1 ounce) of salt in 6 liters (about 1 1/2 gallon) of water, at around 30°C (about 85°F).

Lay the wet, drained skin in the bath. This is called bating the skin. Stir it now and then, often at first. Let the skin lie in the bate 8-12 hours.

Take the skin out; dry it until the moisture is right for scraping. Scrape the flesh side completely free of all membranes. The bate makes it easier than on a raw skin.

On small, thin skins you can usually pull off the membranes with your fingers. Begin at the rump and work your way up toward the head. If the skins are very thin, it may be better to leave a few pieces of membrane than to make a lot of holes.

Dissolve another 200 grams (about 1 1/2 ounces) of alum and 100 grams (about 3/4 ounce) of salt in the old bath. Put the scraped, moist skin back in the bate for 10-12 more hours.

When tanning thin skins the amounts of alum and salt are decreased somewhat, and with coarser skins they may need to be increased.

Flouring, greasing and softening
Furs
Take up the skin, rinse off the wool or fur with water, but avoid rinsing the flesh side. Wring out or centrifuge the skin (eg., in a washing machine on spin cycle). Let the fur dry halfway. The fur is now laid lightly with the flesh side up. Sprinkle a layer of oat or wheat flour over the flesh side {fig. 84}.

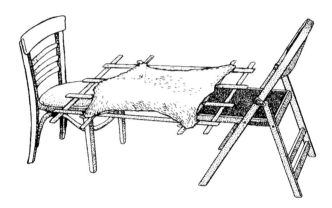

Fig. 84. The skin is put on a grill or on wooden slats, fur side down, and floured.

Do not knead in the flour. Wheat flour gives the finished skin a whiter flesh side. Let the flour lie on the skin 1-2 days. Shake off the flour and soften the skin. If the skin has dried too much, it can be moistened with a little water a couple of hours before beginning the softening.

When the skins have become half-dry they should be greased with, for example, a mixture of 2 egg yolks and a tablespoon of cooking oil.

Dehaired skins
The dehaired skins are hung up to dry and greased when they are half-dry. They are then dried and hung for a week or two before they are moistened and softened.

Preparation of fur with a paste of alum, salt and flour
This method can be used with most fur-skins; I myself have used it on goat, sheep, reindeer and elk skin. For small game skins I recommend the bath method so as not to get paste in the fur, and for hides that lose their hair easily, such as reindeer and elk hides, I recommend this method. The end results are equally good.

Scraping and washing
Scrape the flesh side free of flesh, fat and membranes. Wash the fur [p. 88]. Dried skins to be prepared as furs are first moistened in salted water, 1 dl (about 1/2 cup) salt per 10 liters (about 2 3/4 gallons) water.

Hides from reindeer and elk are not laid in a bath; try to get the fur clean without wetting the whole skin.

Dry the skins until the fur is nearly dry but the flesh side still has a certain amount of moisture and softness. If the flesh side has gotten dirty after washing, scrape it again.

Alum paste
Calculated for a sheepskin:

5 tbsp. alum
1/2 liter (about 1 pint) water
2.5 tbsp. salt
wheat flour

This should be like a viscous paste. Spread out the skin with the flesh side up and spread out the paste in an even coat. Try to get the paste all the way out to the edges without messing up the fur. Fold up the skin with the flesh side in, first along the line of the backbone and then doubled crossways.

Let the folded skin sit at room temperature about 5 days. The time can be shortened somewhat by setting a weight on it. Turn the skin package over after half the time.

To determine whether the skin is completely tanned, one can slice the edge and try to see if the section looks white and firm. If the section is bluish and pasty, then the skin is probably still raw. Remember, though, that the edges are often less thoroughly scraped and are thus the last parts to be tanned through.

The times are calculated for a normal-sized sheepskin. A thinner skin goes faster. If a skin lies many days too long with the paste, then the hairs may begin to fall out. If the paste is on for too short a time, then it is hard to get it soft; the raw areas also dry much more slowly.

Softening and greasing
Unfold the skin and let the paste dry a bit. Scrape off the paste and dry and soften the skin. When the skin is half dry, it should be fat liquored with, for example, a mixture of 2 egg yolks and a tablespoon of cooking oil.

Glacé tanning
Glacé tanning yields a soft, elastic and bright leather that is primarily used for gloves. The skins that are glacé tanned to the greatest extent are

young lamb and goatskin. Dehairing with lime, puering and bran bating, as described on pp. 58-62.

Tanning
Glacé bate for a kid- or lamb-skin:

50 grams (about 1/3 ounce) flour	2 egg yolks
25 grams (about 1/6 ounce) alum	1 tsp. olive oil
10 grams (about 1/15 ounce) salt	1 dl (about 1/2 cup) water

Mix the flour and a little of the water into a smooth paste. Mix the egg yolks with a little lukewarm water and add the olive oil. Dissolve the alum and salt in the rest of the water and add first the flour paste and then the egg and oil mixture. The mixture should be at a temperature of 35 °C (95°F). Lay the skin in a bucket with the bate and work it at regular intervals until the tanning is complete, which takes 2-3 hours.

Finishing
Hang up the skin without wringing it out and let it dry. The result is best if it is left to hang for a few weeks before softening.

Then moisten the skin by spraying it with water from a plant sprayer and put it in a plastic bag for several hours. Soften by staking [see Fig. 89, p.98].

Glazing
Glazing involves scrubbing the grain side so that it becomes shiny and tight. For extra shine, the dry and soft skin is smeared on the grain side with egg white which is allowed to harden, after which the skin is glazed with a sleeker {fig. 82, p. 86}. The skins can also be glazed by being pulled over the stake; make sure the edges of the stake are even and smooth.

Bate of oat flour, salt and water
When the Malung tanners went from farm to farm and processed skins or sewed pelts, it was common for the skins to have been bated beforehand. Bated skins are easier to scrape and to make soft than those that are prepared fresh, but they develop a strong acid smell that remains for a time after they are prepared.

I got this recipe from Perjos Lars Halvarsson of Heden, Lima. [Dalarna, Sweden.] The raw skin is washed and dried before it is laid in the bate, which consists of a double handful of oat flour and a fistful of salt per skin {fig. 85, p. 92}.

Fig. 85. *The amount of flour that can be held in a pair of cupped hands.*

Dissolve the salt in hot water, the flour in cold water, and then beat the flour mix into the salt solution. The finished bate should have a temperature of around 35°C (95°F). Lay the skins down with the flesh side up, the topmost one with the fur up. Lay a few boards over the top and press the skins down until they are completely covered by the bate. Every other day, take the skins up and lay them down again, with the skin that was on the top now at the bottom. If the bate is warmed up at the same time, so-called warm bating, the preparations take 12-14 days. Cold bating, that is without warming, takes about 1 month.

After a day or so the bate begins to ferment; organic acids are formed such as lactic and acetic acid. These acids have a preservative effect on the skin. The skins are fully bated when the wool and epidermis in the groin area can be scraped away easily.

Hang the bated skins up to dry. In this condition the wool is loose; for this reason, you should not pull on the wool or wring out the skin. The wool will become anchored again as the skin dries. Let the skins hang until they are fully dry, then moisten them a little and scrape them clean of fat and membranes, which are now much looser than they were before bating. Stretch the skins until they are dry and soft.

All that is left is to beat the flour out of the wool, which can be pretty hard work.

Urine tanning chemistry

Within the leather trade, urine has been used for dehairing skins, for tanning skins and for washing skins. Urine contains formic acid, urinase, and uric acid, among other things. These acids have a preservative effect on the skin. When urine is left to stand ammonia is formed, which is a strong base. If a hide sits in urine for some time, the basic environment will begin to have a dehairing effect.

Ammonia influences the skin by splitting the naturally occurring fats, to form glycerol and free fatty acids. These free fatty acids can penetrate the hide and react with the fibers of the dermis; the skin is tanned. When ammonia is used as a cleaning liquid, it is it's saponifying properties that are being exploited.

I have made a few tries at urine tanning of fish skin. The recipes I started with come from Rita Pitka Blumenstein, who lives on Nelson Island in southwestern Alaska. She relates the following:

"Fishskins were used for mukluks, mittens, water carriers, and rain-coats....The king salmon is used for boots, heavy-duty boots. Only female silver salmon is used for hats for girls. And the pike skin is for water jugs. The trout is for bags....

"You take the skin off and soak it in the water, and then you scrape it with a sea shell. Some fish you have to scale; some fish you don't. Like pike and white fish, you've got to scale it; you soak it in urine. The urine has to come from a young boy baby before weaning. It doesn't contain any chemicals, just momma's milk. For thicker skins, you have to use the urine from an older boy, around the time his voice changes.

"[The skin soaks in the urine] sometimes half a day, sometimes over-night. The longer you soak it, the softer it gets. Then my mother used to use [Fells] Naphtha soap, and she sudsed it in the water and then cooled off the water and then put the skin in it. Then she puts aspen shavings in the water and cools it off, then you rinse it in clear water and wring it out. My mother used a towel to absorb the water. I asked her one time in camp, 'What did you use when you didn't have cloth?' She said they used dried moss. And then you put it on a smooth board, stick it there, the inside facing in. Then when it dries, it will just peel off it-self. You store it away, and when you are ready to use it, you wet the shavings that you saved, and you pad them onto the fishskin on the outer side. Then you roll it and leave it until it dries. Then you shake it off." [Hickman 1988: 19ff.]

I have started from this recipe but have used woman's urine for 10-12 hours and then rinsed the skins, washed them in water with soap, laid them in a willow bark bath 10-12 hours, greased them with, for example, train oil, dried them and softened them.

"Moors" was the name primarily for the Arabs who came to Spain from North Africa during the middle ages.

DYEING

The dyeing of leather has old roots, to judge from finds from Egypt (among other places) where it was discovered early on that certain plant juices could give pretty colors. Some of the plants that can dye also contain tannins and it has been debated whether dyeing or tanning came first.

Dyeing alum-tanned leather

It is easiest to dye leather that has been tanned with alum, and I usually use the recipes found in books on wool dying with plant materials. Keep in mind that the temperature at which the skins are laid in the dye should not exceed 38°C (about 100°F); instead, let the skins soak for a longer time. The colors are not as fast as in wool dyeing and they have a tendency to run. The dyeing can be done in two different ways:

1. Boil the dye bath and mix in alum and salt in the same quantities as the recipe on p. 87 prescribes. Tanning and dying will happen at the same time.

2. Tan the skin in an alum bath, dry and soften it but do not grease it. Boil the dye bath, let it cool down and then rub the side of the skin that is to be tanned with a sponge dipped in the dye bath. Let the dye dry in and repeat the process until you have the desired color.

Oil the skin after dyeing.

Chamois leather

Chamois leather can also be dyed with vegetable dyes. Tan the leather, dry it and soften it before putting it in the dye bath. If the skins feel dry then grease them again after dyeing with, for example, egg yolk.

Dyeing bark tanned leather.

From the Sami we know about pretty red-brown reindeer skins. The red-brown color comes from the inner bark of the alder tree.

The strongest dye comes from the bark of the roots if it is taken in the wintertime. Let the bark dry and then grind it in a nut-mill or pulverize it in another way, for example by chewing it. Mix the pulverized bark with hot water and a little soap to get a pulp. When the pulp has cooled, rub it into the leather to the desired color and let it dry. Brush the skin with a soft brush.

Different methods have been used to strengthen the dye, for example bloodroot (*Potentilla erecta*) or red ochre, from the bogs. Oil the skin after dyeing.

Black skins

Tannins together with iron salts [ferrous sulfate/copperas/green vitriol] produce black colors, a reaction which is also used in the production of ink. Craft tanners often keep a thin bark liquor or small beer standing with an old piece of scrap iron in it. The tanned skins were rubbed with the mixture several times over until they reached the desired color.

Leather blackened with iron-black will fade over time, and an excess of iron can make the grain fragile.

Other materials used to get black skins are copper sulfate (blue vitriol), lamp-black, soot, and Brazil wood. Oil the skin after dyeing.

Oiling

During tanning, the skins' natural fats have, for the most part, disappeared. To get a soft and supple leather, fat must be supplied between the fibers of the hide to keep them separate and let them glide across each other. A number of different substances have been used to lubricate leather. Train oil, tallow, neatsfoot oil, butter, industrial olive oil (a by-product of olive oil production), and rape oil are examples.

Egg yolk is a valued lubricant for white skins, because skins lubricated with egg yolk do not turn yellow. Sheep tallow, as well as a mixture of tallow and tar, make the leather water-resistant.

By mixing soft fats, like tallow, with hard ones, for example stearine or paraffin, a harder and firmer leather was produced, useful for straps among other things.

When the hide has been stretched out in all directions, the fur on pelts has begun to dry and the flesh side has an even level of moisture, then it is time to grease the skin. If the hide has an uneven moisture content, the fat will be drawn in unevenly and the finished leather will be spotted. It is better to have the skin a little too wet than too dry.

Grease thin hides first on the grain side. If a thin skin is greased first on the flesh side, the fat can be drawn in and make spots on the grain side. When the fat has penetrated and the skin has dried a little, then grease the flesh side.

Oil bark tanned hides with train oil on the grain side and a mixture of equal parts train oil and tallow on the flesh side. Thin skins can be greased with train oil on both sides or with the same fats as alum-tawed skins.

Oil alum-tawed leather and alumned furs with a mixture of 1/2 dl (about 1/4 cup) olive oil, 1/2 dl (about 1/4 cup) water and a teaspoon of soap, or 2 egg yolks, 1/2 dl (about 1/4 cup) water and a tablespoon of oil (olive or cooking oil). Chamois leather, and thin skins that feel dry and rough, should be treated with egg yolk.

Fig 45a, scraping the flesh side with an elk bone (see p. 50.)

SOFTENING

When the hide has dried somewhat but has not begun to stiffen, it is time to begin the softening process that then continues until the hide is dry and soft. The hide must be worked at regular intervals throughout the drying. The collagen fibers must be stretched out to make the hide soft and supple.

Always begin by softening the edges; otherwise you run the risk of getting a skin with a pouch in the middle, because the stretching has nowhere to go but is stopped by the hard edges.

It is important to work the hide both lengthwise and crosswise so as not to get an unnaturally long and narrow skin or pelt. Softening can be done many different ways:

a) On a scraping rack {fig. 41, p. 48}, in the same manner as with scraping, but with duller tools.
b) If the hide is stretched out on a frame {fig. 44, p. 50}, you can beat the hide and tighten the cords to make the hide stretch.
c) Drawing osier
   {fig. 86a and 86b}.
d) Leather hook
   {fig. 88}.
e) Stake {fig. 89}.
f) Graining board
   {fig. 90}.
g) Tumbling drum
   {fig. 91}.
h) Rubbing with
   the hands.

Fig. 86a: Drawing cane, made of iron.

Fig. 86b: Drawing cane made of a birch or fir branch that grew crooked, with crosswise grooves sawn into it. A sturdy rope, a twisted osier switch or a chain/cable can also be used as a drawing cane. Pull the hides back and forth. This works for pelts, leather and chamois leather. When softening larger hides, it may be simpler if two people cooperate, each pulling from opposite sides.

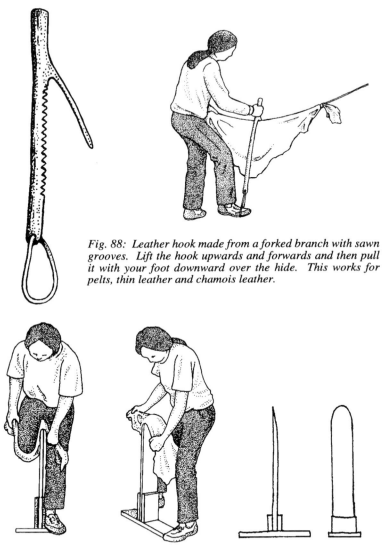

Fig. 88: Leather hook made from a forked branch with sawn grooves. Lift the hook upwards and forwards and then pull it with your foot downward over the hide. This works for pelts, thin leather and chamois leather.

Fig. 89: Wooden stake. Pull the skin back and forth over the end of the post. Used primarily for thinner skins. For extra force, you can press on it with one knee.

98

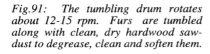

Fig. 90: Wooden graining board. The bottom can be grooved or made of cork. Move a pleat in the hide forward and back with the help of the graining board. Used primarily for thick hides.

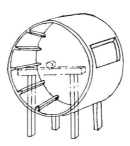

Fig.91: The tumbling drum rotates about 12-15 rpm. Furs are tumbled along with clean, dry hardwood sawdust to degrease, clean and soften them.

WASHING

Untanned furs can be washed with soap, oil & soap [see below] or shampoo. If the fur is spotted with blood, put the skin first in cold water for a while. Then gradually raise the temperature in the following baths until you get up to 35°C (95°F). Sheepskin gets tangled easily, especially if you change it between hot and cold water. Wash very dirty skins first in oil & soap and then in soap or shampoo. Shampoo gives the fur a pretty shine.

Do not let the skin sit in the wash-water until it cools. The warm wash-water dissolves grease and dirt out of the pelt; when the bath cools down, the grease goes back into the fur and is then harder to remove.

Sheepskins often need many washings and rinses before they are clean. Sheep and goat-skins can be spun dry. Put the skin in a pillowcase to protect the centrifuge. *[Swedes often use a centrifuge as a clothes-drier instead of the hot-air tumbler common in the U.S. - Trans.]*

Very sensitive skins, like reindeer and moose, should be washed carefully on the hair side without being submerged into the bath.

Oil & soap is used like regular soap and is made up as needed from:

4 dl (about 1 3/4 cups) water
2 dl (about 7/8 cup) household ammonia
1 dl (about 1/2 cup) oleic acid

Tanned hides and furs
Fat liquored hides and furs
Wash in soapy water. If you put a little soap in the last rinse water, it will be easier to soften hides that have stiffened while drying.
Vegetable-tanned leather
Method **A**. Wash in warm water and soap. Put 1/2 dl (about 1/4 cup) olive oil and a pat of soap in the last rinse water to fat liquor.
Method **B**. Boil 2 tbsp. linseed in 1/2 liter (about 1 pint) water for 15 mins. Filter out the linseeds. Rub into what you want to wash. Let stand overnight. Wipe clean with a rag.

Iron spots on vegetable tanned skins can be bleached by dissolving 1 part oxalic acid powder in 10 parts water and brushing onto the spot; rinse well.
Alum tawed hides and furs
These don't stand up to washing well, especially when newly-tawed. Wash in as little water as possible, since the alum dissolves in the water until the water and the skin have the same alum content. Wash with soap or shampoo. An alum-tawed skin can be tawed again.

Wild skins are dried by rubbing hardwood sawdust into the wet pelt. The most effective treatment is drying the skin in a tumbling drum, a rotating drum with dry sawdust {Fig. 91}. Shake and comb out the fur.

GLUE

Glue-leather is the name for the scraps of hide that are left when hides are sliced, pared or scraped clean after liming and dehairing. The collagen in the hide changes easily to glue if it is basic, that is, dehaired with lime or ashes [Skans, 1990: 148]. The glue scraps are left in a heap and left to dry until the day set aside for cooking the glue.

The tanner Arvid Kalkstrand from Fåker in Jämtland relates: "We got up early and began to boil the glue-leather around four in the morning. The glue-leather was mixed with a lot of water and boiled all day. In the evening we strained the liquid and poured it in a wooden vat, where it cooled into a quivery mass, that was then sliced with a taut steel wire into thin slices. The slices were dried on a net and sold." When the glue is to be used, the sheet glue is dissolved in warm water.

PARCHMENT

This is how the master singer and shoemaker Hans Sachs
described parchment making in Nuremberg in the 16th century.
The verse is illustrated by the copper engraver Jost Amman {fig. 92}.

Ich kauff Schaffell, Boeck, uñ die Geiß,
Die Fell leg ich denn in die beyß,
Darnach firm ich sie sauber rein,
Spann auff die Ram jeds Fell allein,
Schabs darnach, mach Permennt darauß,
Mit grosser arbeit in mein Hauß,
Auß ohrn und klauwen seud ich Leim,
Das alles verkauff ich daheim. *

(I buy sheep-skins, ram and goat,
The skins I lay then in the bate,
And then I make them pure and clean,
Stretch on the frame each skin alone,
Scrape it then, make parchment of it,
With hard work in my house,
From the ears and the hooves I boil glue,
I sell it all at home.)

Fig. 92. Parchmentmaker

From: The Book of Trades [Ständebuch], *Jost Amman & Hans Sachs, with
a new introduction by Benjamin A. Rifkin (New York: Dover, 1973), p. 101].*

The word parchment [pergament] probably comes from the city of Pergamon in Asia Minor. Pergamon was an important center of Hellenic culture, known for its architecture and its art.

According to Pliny the Elder*, a library was founded in Pergamon around 200 B.C. This library became too strong a competitor for the famous library of Alexandria; out of jealousy, the Egyptian pharaoh forbade the export of papyrus. Egypt was at that time the center of papyrus production and the one place where usable papyrus-reeds grew.

The writers of Pergamon were forced to look for a substitute. Leather was already used to write on, but the method was refined and Pergamon became the center of parchment manufacture.

The oldest surviving documents written on leather are actually much older than this; they come from Egypt's XIIth Dynasty, 1991-1786 B.C. The oldest known parchment was found in Israel and dated to about 800 B.C. [Frendrup 1989: 13].

The Dead Sea Scrolls, a collection of texts and textual fragments in Hebrew and Aramaic, found in 1947 in mountain caves to the northwest of the Dead Sea, are probably the most famous documents on leather preserved from antiquity. They come from the period 200 B.C. to 70 A.D. [*Bra Böckers lexicon*].

Parchment has been made from skins of sheep, goat, calf, and deer; in fact, any fur-bearing animal. If you want white parchment, you must use only skins from animals with white fur.

We know how parchment was made in Europe in the 12th century from Theophilus Presbyter in the following recipe:

"Take goatskins and stand them in water for a day and a night. Take them and wash them until the water runs clear. Take an entirely new bath and place therein old lime (*calcem non recentem*) and water mixing well together to form a thick cloudy liquor. Place the skins into this, folding them on the flesh side. Move them with a pole two or three times each day, leaving them for eight days (and twice as long as winter).

"Next you must withdraw the skins and unhair them. Pour off the contents of the bath and repeat the process using the same quantities, placing the skins in the lime liquor and moving them once each day over eight days as before.

"Then take them out and wash them well until the water runs quite clean. Place them in another bath with clean water and leave them for two days.

"Then take them out, attach the cords and tie them to the circular frame. Dry, then shave them with a sharp knife, after which, leave for two days out of the sun ... moisten with water and rub the flesh side with powdered pumice. After two days wet it again by sprinkling with a little water and fully clean the flesh side with pumice so as to make it quite wet again. Then tighten up the cords, equalise the tension so that the sheet will become permanent. Once the sheets are dry, nothing further remains to be done." [Reed 1972: 133f]

By drying the parchment stretched tight in a frame, the collagen fibers are made to arrange themselves parallel to the surface in different layers, which means that the finished parchment can be split into several thin sheets {Fig. 93}. If the skin is not exposed to liquid or too much humidity, the parchment will keep its shape for a very long time.

For further reading and study of parchment I recommend:

Nature and Making of Parchment, R. Reed. Elmete Press, 1975.

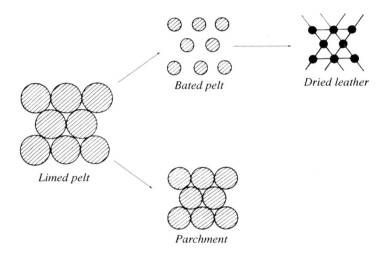

Fig. 93: Diagram to show different spatial arrangement of collagen fibres in leather and parchment [Reed 1972: 123].

Pliny the Elder, Gaius Plinius Secundus, 27-79 A.D., a Roman civil servant and writer. His only surviving work is Naturalis Historia, *an encyclopedia of 37 volumes [Bra Böckers lexicon].*

DIFFERENT VARIETIES OF LEATHER

Box-calf is chromium tanned, dyed calfskin. After tanning, dyeing and greasing, the skins are dried so that they become hard and stiff. The skins are re-moisturized in boxes of moist sawdust; hence the name.

Chevreau, originally a glacé-tanned goatskin (chevreau is French for goat), is nowadays a chromium tanned goat or horseskin, called horse chevreau.

Chevrette is made the same way as chevreau, but from sheepskin.

Cordovan leather was made mostly from goatskins and got its name from the Spanish city of Cordova. The vegetable-tanned skins appeared in many different colors, with smooth or patterned grain.

Cordovan leather is a compact and watertight sport leather, made from horse's butt that is chromium or combination-tanned (chromium and vegetable tanning). [*This is called cordovan in Swedish; the other one I translate above as "cordovan" is called karduan in Swedish.--trans.*]

Distressed grain. The skins are grainy and streaked on the grain side, a surface that historically was produced in the Orient by pressing small seeds into the grain. In Europe the pattern was pressed in with plates or rollers. Finally, the skin was crushed with the crushing-board.

Dongola tanning is named for a province in Nubia. The tanning is done mostly on calfskin that has been prepared in alum, salt and catechu, an extract of wood from the Acacia catechu, and then tanned with sumac or other vegetable tannins.

Grain-leather was made from cow and other bovine hides and was used as upper-leather for heavy shoes; the hides were bark-tanned and the wet hides were greased on the grain and flesh sides with a mixture of tallow and train oil. The hides were left lying in piles for 1-2 months until the water had evaporated and been replaced by the fat, producing a tight and compact leather.

Lacquer-leather, originally vegetable-tanned leather that was lacquered on the flesh side with warm lacquer made by heating linseed oil together with a drying agent. Today it is made of chromium tanned leather whose grain is polished and lacquered.

Nappa tanning is a combination of alum and vegetable tanning, used primarily for glove leather.

Ross-leather is made of vegetable tanned horsehide. Ross means horse.

Russian leather was originally only prepared in Russia; it had an unusual smell along with strength and suppleness, and appeared mostly as either red or black. It was made from large cowhides, horses, calves and goats. The skins were tanned with bark and alum, dyed and saturated with birch oil, which gave them their special smell. The oil was made by dry distillation of birch-bark from birches standing on sandy soil, that had decayed so much that the bark was nearly all that remained.

Saffian leather, also called morocco, got its names from the city of Saffi in Morocco, and is sumac tanned goat or sheepskin. Red saffian was considered the finest of leathers.

Suede, a glacé-tanned goat or lambskin that is polished on the flesh side to get a velvety surface. Nowadays it is most often a chromium tanned calfskin with a polished flesh side.

Swedish leather was made with a combination of alum and vegetable tanning and was used for making Swedish gloves, or *Gants de Suède.* The leather was polished on the flesh side, which was worn outwards.

Wax leather was made from grain leather that was cleaned thoroughly on the flesh side, which was worn flesh out.

SHOPPING LIST
Drugstore
Alum
Oleic acid
Oxalic acid powder
Cod-liver oil (more expensive than fodder-train oil, but has the same effect)
Farmers/veterinary supplier
Fodder-train oil
Coarse salt
Paint shop
Spackling knives
Alum
Oxalic acid powder
Van Dykes
Woonsocket, SD 57385
Tanning tools such as scrapers, scraping spades, stakes, and knives.
Supplier of tanning fats, alum, etc., in small quantities.

STUDY PLAN
Introduction

Working with a study circle involves possibilities for increased knowledge, personal development and companionship with other people. Since everyone in the group has something to contribute, you reach a high degree of knowledge and get an exchange of experiences that cannot be found through conventional schooling.

For satisfactory results, strong demands are placed on the group leader and course material. The group leader functions as a team manager and has the job of bringing out the core of the study material and prompting the participants so that everyone's knowledge and experiences are taken into account.

The participants' active involvement in the circle is thus important.

It is essential that the group work out together how the course material should be structured, what is important and what is less important. This should be done at the first meeting.

The participants in the circle should have this basic text, *Leather: Tanning and Preparation by Traditional Methods* (The Caber Press, ISBN 1-887719-00-8).

Setting goals:
The aim is to preserve and further develop knowledge of the traditional and natural methods that have been used to tan and prepare leather.
Participants should, at the end of the course, be able to tan and prepare their own hides and skins.

Planning:
The circle starts with alum tawing of furs and then continues with bark tanning and oil tanning.
It is difficult to always have the same meeting time. The skins can be quicker or slower to be ready for the next step in the tanning process, and a bit of adjustment may be required between the meetings.
To start off every meeting there should be a discussion of what happened at the previous meeting, and whether any participants have thoughts about that. Then there should be a theoretical introduction
before the group starts in with practical work.

Field trips:
Leather shops, tanneries and museums.

Suggested reading:
Belitz, Larry: *Brain Tanning the Sioux Way* (Hot Springs, SD, 1987).

Churchill, James: *The Complete Book of Tanning Skins and Furs* (Harrisburg, PA, 1983).

Mason, Otis: "Aboriginal Skin-Dressing," reproduced from: *Smithsonian Annual Report 1889* (published in 1891); reprinted by the Shorey Book Store, Seattle, WA, various reprints, from 1971.

McPherson, John: *Brain Tan Buckskin* (Randolph, KS, 1986).

White, George M.: *Craft Manual of North American Indian Footwear* (Ronan, MT, 1969).

Wilder, Edna: *Secrets of Eskimo Skin Sewing* (Anchorage, AK, 1976).

Suggested films:
Russell and Yvonne Willier *Brain-tan a Moose Skin.*
Available from: Centre for the Cross-Cultural Study of Health and Healing, Dept. of Anthropology, Univ. of Alberta, Edmonton T6G 2H4

"Inuiternas sätt at bereda ren- och sälskinn" *[How the Inuits Prepare Skin from Reindeer and Sealskin]*(30 min.) Dag Hartman/Lotta Rahme, 1989. (Romo Film Produktion; Romo 1076; c/o Lotta's Garfveri: Langgatn 9, S-19330 Sweden Phone: 468-592-55000].

"Indiansk sämskskinnsgarvning"*[Indian Brain Tanning]* (30 min.) Dag Hartman/Lotta Rahme, 1989. (Romo Film Produktion).

"Skinn och läder, en film om barkgarvning"[Skin and Leather; *(Film about Bark Tanning]* (25 min.) Karleby Hembygdsmuseum 1971. (Karleby Stadshuset; Johan Helander; Salutorget 1; 671 01 Karleby; Sweden; phone 009358/68/2891).

"Malunsskinnare" *[Tanner's from Malung]* (b/w, 60 min.) (Rent from Malung Library; Fack 94; 782 31 Malung; Sweden; phone 0280/183 00).

"Samisk hemgarvning och sömnad av en kaffepåse." *[How the Sami People Tan Skins and Sew a Coffee Bag]* (295 min.) Filmed at the home of Maja Nilsson; Lövberg, Vilhelmina, 1964. (Västerrbottens museum; 902 34 Umeå; Sweden; phone 090/118635).

Meeting 1:
The leader and participants introduce themselves; besides names etc., it is good to discuss what expectations everyone has of the study circle, whether anyone has had previous experiences with tanning, and such.

The leader outlines the purpose of the study circle and skims through the book together with the participants. Afterwards, an agreement is reached on the goals of the circle.

Working out of practical questions, for example time and place for field trips, assistance of experts, as well as the schedule of the circle: dates, times and places for the different meetings. Which skins, tools and materials should be acquired.

For the next meeting: read pp. 1-29 and 43-53.

Meeting 2:
Discuss history: how and why people began preparing leather, similarities and differences between today and 10,000, 2000 and 100 years ago.

Differences and similarities between the Inuit, Indian and Sami ways of taking care of and working hides, skins and pelts.

Reviewing the various tools needed and an introductory description of how to make different tools, scraping racks, scrapers etc.

For the next meeting: read pp. 30-42, 54-62, 87-93 and 100, and make a tool if needed.

Meeting 3:
Discuss the benefits and drawbacks of alum tawing.
Scrape and wash skins to be alum tawed.
For the next meeting: read pp. 87-91 and 94-99.

Meeting 4:
Discuss which scrapers are best. Angles of sharpened edges.

What did people use before iron? Continue scraping if needed. Begin alum-tawing with bath or paste. Skins prepared according to the recipe [p. 88] should be hung up after 10-12 hours and scraped, the bath strengthened, and the skin laid back in. After another 10-12 hours take the skin up, rinse the fur and let the skin drain before flouring the flesh side.
For the next meeting: read pp. 78-86; some people are appointed responsible for completing the alum-preparation.

Meeting 5:
Discuss which skins should be bark-tanned and how to get the bark. Prepare for dehairing.
Grease and begin softening the alum-tawed skins.

Meeting 6:
Discuss the benefits and drawbacks of bark-tanning.
Dehair the skins, boil the bark-liquor.
Put the skins in the first bark-liquor.
Bark-tanning requires a lot of care, stirring and strengthening of the bark-liquor; appoint people to be responsible.
Continue softening the alum-tawed skins.
For the next meeting: read pp. 63-77.

Meeting 7:
Take the skins out of the bark-bath and scrape them; strengthen the liquor.
Discuss what skins will be oil tanned with fur and without fur; begin scraping the flesh side.

Meeting 8:
Discuss the benefits and drawbacks of oil tanning.
Prepare for dehairing of the skins that are to be oil tanned without fur.
Greasing and softening of the bark-tanned skins.
For the next meeting: read pp. 20-22, 65-68 and 70-77.

Meeting 9:
Discuss the differences between the Swedish and Indian oil tanning methods.
Skins to be oil tanned should be dehaired, scraped and greased.
The oil tanned skins are worked regularly until the next meeting.
For the next meeting: appoint people to be responsible for working the oil tanned skins.

Meeting 10:
Discuss what softening entails and how to proceed for different skins.
Wash the oil tanned skins. Begin softening.
For the next meeting: read pp. 75-77, 91-93 and 101-106.

Meeting 11:
Discuss the benefits and drawbacks of smoke-tanning.
Finish softening the oil tanned skins, smoking if needed.

Meeting 12:
Discussions about the finished skins, comparisons of home-tanned and industrially-tanned leather.

Last meeting:
At the last meeting it is important to go back and see how the goals and expectations of the study circle have been fulfilled..

Bibliography

Austin, William E. *Principles and Practice of Fur Dressing and Fur Dyeing.* D. Van Nostrand Co., New York, 1922.

Barber, Elizabeth W. *Women's Work: the First 20,000 Years.* W.W. Norton & Co. New York, 1994.

Bogoras, W. The Chukchee. *The Jesup North Pacific Expedition,* Vol. VII. USA, 1975.

Cram, J.M. and Cram, D.J. *The Essence of Organic Chemistry.* Addison-Wesley Publishing Co. Massachusetts, 1979.

Diaconus, P. *Lanogobardernas Historia.* Uddevalla, 1971.

Ehrnberg, G. & Hemberg, S. *Läderberedningen och des Historia.* Hantverksinstitutets Yrkeshandböcker. Ser. Materialkunskap No. 15. Kristianstad, 1924.

Farnham, A.B. *Home Tanning and Leathermaking Guide.* Columbus, Ohio, 1950.

Forbes, R.J. *Studies in Ancient Technology.* Vol. V. Netherlands, 1957.

Fries, G.E. *Indian Pioneer and Home Tanning Methods.* Iowa, 1977.

Frendrup, W. *Bemærkninger Vedrørende Garvningens Historie.* Dansk Konserveringspersonals Fællesudvalg, 1989.

Gansser, A. The Early History of Tanning. *Ciba Review 81.* Basel, 1950.
Gidmark, D. *The Indian Crafts.* Canada, 1980.

Gustavson, K.H. *The Chemistry of Tanning Processes.* Academic Press, Inc., New York, 1956.

Hald, Margrethe. *Ancient Danish Textiles From Bogs and Burial.* Copenhagen, 1980.

Handbook of Chemistry and Physics. 1979/80. Florida, 1979.

Hungry Wolf, A. *Traditional Dress Issue.* Good Medicine Books. British Columbia, 1971.

110

International Glossary of Leather Terms. International Council of Tanners, London, 1968.

Kellog, Kathy. *Home Tanning & Leathercraft Simplified.* Williamson Pub. Co. Charlotte, Vermont, 1984.

Lagerlöf, E. & Bendz, G. Homeros' Iliad. Malmö, Sweden, 1958.

Lamb, M.C. *Leather Dressing.* The Leather Trades Publishing Co., London, 1909.

Larrson, A. *Konservering og Restaurering af Læder, Skind og Pergament.* Lund, 1978.

Lehninger, A.L. *Biochemistry.* Worth Publishers, Inc. New York, 1976.

MacIntosh, T. *Moose Hair Tufting and Porcupine Quillwork.* Native Woman's Association of the NWT, Yellowknife. nd.

Mason, O.T. Aboriginal Skin Dressing. *Annual Report of the Board of Regents of the Smithsonian Institute.* Washington, 1891.

McKennan, R.A. *The Chandalar Kutchin.* Arctic Institute of North America Technical Paper No. 17. Canada, 1965.

Morenus, R. *The Hudson's Bay Company.* Toronto, 1956.

Nesheim, A. the Lapp Fur and Skin Terminology and its Historical Background. *Studia Ethnographica Upsaliensia XXI.* Lapponica, 1964. pp. 199-218, Lund, Sweden.

Mowat, F. *People of the Deer.* London, 1952.

Oakes, J.E. *Factors Influencing Kamik Production in Arctic Bay, NWT.* Canadian Ethnology Service, paper No. 107. Canada, 1987.

O'Flaherty, F., Roddy, W.T., & Lollar, R.M. *The Chemistry and Technology of Leather.* Vols. I & 2. London, 1956, 58.

O'Flaherty, F. "Salt: Its Role in Cure." *The Leather Manufacturer,* November, 1961.

Procter, H.R. *The Principles of Leather Manufacture.* E. & F.N. Spon, Ltd., London, 1936.

Rahme, L. *Garvning och Beredning av Hudar och Skinn med Traditionella Metoder.* Institutet för Förhistorisk Teknologi. Nr. 11. Sveg, 1985.

Rahme, L. *Skinnkläder.* B-Uppsats i Arkeologi. Uppsala Univ., 1987.

111

Ray, P.M. *The Living Plant.* Holt Reinhart and Winston, Inc. New York, 1972.

Reed, R. *Ancient Skins, Parchments and Leathers.* Seminar Press. London and New York, 1972.

Rose, C.L. & Von Endt, D.W., eds. *Protein Chemistry for Conservators.* A.I.C., Washington, D.C., 1984.

Rosing, J. *The Sky Hangs Low.* Ontario, 1979.

Salaman, R.A. *Dictionary of Leather-Working Tools, c. 1700-1950.* Macmillan Publ. Co., New York, 1986.

Salisbury, F.B. and Ross, C.W. *Plant Physiology.* Wadsworth Publishing Co., Inc. California, 1978.

Santappa, M. and Sundara Rao, V.S. Vegetable Tannins: a Review. *Journal of Scientific and Industrial Research,* Vol. 41, December, 1982. pp. 705-718.

Schneider, R.C. *Crafts of the North American Indian.* A Craftman's Manual. Wisconsin, 1972.

Sharphouse, J.H. Theory and Practice of Modern Chamois Leather Production. *Journal of the Society of Leather Technologists and Chemists,* Vol. 69, pp. 29-43.

Shuttleworth, S.G. The Mechanism of Vegetable Tannage. *Journal of the American Leather Chemists Association,* Vol. 47. 1952, pp. 603-622.

Tanning in the United States to 1850: A Brief History. Washington, D.C.: Smithsonian Institution. 1964.

Thompson, J. *Pride of the Indian Wardrobe.* Canada, 1990.

Thorstensen, T.C. *Practical Leather Technology.* Van Nostrand Reinhold Co. New York, 1969.

Tsai, L.S. and Wilson, E.O. Smoke Tannage. *Journal of the American Leather Chemists Association*, Vol. XXIV. Easton, PA, 1929.

van de Velde, P. *Analecta Praehistorica Leidensia*, Vol VI. Rituals, Skins and Homer. The Danubian Tanpits. 1973.

Waterer, J.W. *Leather Craftsmanship.* London, 1968.

Waterer, J.W. Leather. *A History of Technology*, Vol. II. 1956, pp. 147-190.

Internet sites of interest: http://braintan.com
http://ic.net/~tbailey/primitive.html